T0319076

# Cambridge Elements ≡

Elements in the Philosophy of Immanuel Kant
edited by
Desmond Hogan
*Princeton University*
Howard Williams
*University of Cardiff*
Allen Wood
*Indiana University*

# KANT'S POWER OF IMAGINATION

Rolf-Peter Horstmann
*Humboldt Universität zu Berlin*

CAMBRIDGE
UNIVERSITY PRESS

# CAMBRIDGE
## UNIVERSITY PRESS

University Printing House, Cambridge CB2 8BS, United Kingdom

One Liberty Plaza, 20th Floor, New York, NY 10006, USA

477 Williamstown Road, Port Melbourne, VIC 3207, Australia

314–321, 3rd Floor, Plot 3, Splendor Forum, Jasola District Centre,
New Delhi – 110025, India

79 Anson Road, #06–04/06, Singapore 079906

Cambridge University Press is part of the University of Cambridge.

It furthers the University's mission by disseminating knowledge in the pursuit of education, learning, and research at the highest international levels of excellence.

www.cambridge.org
Information on this title: www.cambridge.org/9781108464031
DOI: 10.1017/9781108565066

First published 2018

*A catalogue record for this publication is available from the British Library.*

ISBN 978-1-108-46403-1 Paperback
ISSN 2397-9461 (online)
ISSN 2514-3824 (print)

Cambridge University Press has no responsibility for the persistence or accuracy of URLs for external or third-party internet websites referred to in this publication and does not guarantee that any content on such websites is, or will remain, accurate or appropriate.

# Contents

# Kant's Power of Imagination

Rolf-Peter Horstmann

**Abstract:** *This Element is a study of how the power of imagination is, according to Kant, supposed to contribute to cognition. It is meant to be an immanent and a reconstructive endeavor, relying solely on Kant's own resources when he tries to determine what material, faculties, and operations are necessary for cognition of objects. The discourse is divided into two sections. The first deals with Kant's views concerning the power of imagination as outlined in the A- and B-editions of the* Critique of Pure Reason. *The second focuses on the power of imagination in the first part of the* Critique of Judgment.

**Keywords:** *Epistemology*

**ISSNs:** *2397–9461 (online), 2514–3824 (print)*

**ISBNs:** *9781108464031 (PB), 9781108565066 (OC)*

## Introduction

"Thoughts are hard to come by."                    (Anonymous)

Not many topics in Kant's theoretical philosophy have captured the imagination of Kant scholars as vividly as his conception of the power of imagination. It is not as if Kant scholars particularly enjoy indulging in the exercise of "representing an object without its presence in intuition" (*CpR*, B 151),[1] though this might sometimes be a recommendable exercise, even for Kant scholars. Rather, this conception captures their imagination because they cannot imagine what on earth led Kant to think that his doctrine of the power of imagination contributes anything valuable to his otherwise elegant attempt to reconcile conceptual and nonconceptual, active and passive, intellectual and sensual elements in his account of knowledge and experience. When having to deal with Kant's ideas about the mechanisms and achievements of the imagination in the context of his epistemology, most Kant scholars behave as we all supposedly behave in the face of fantasies and dreams: they either repress the whole topic, as if Kant could as well have done without it, or aggressively blame Kant for willfully making his epistemology more obscure than it needed to be.[2]

Now, one must admit that these two attitudes are not unfounded, that they are even encouraged by what Kant says about the power of imagination. Even if one focuses on the first two editions of the *Critique of Pure Reason* (*CpR*) and the *Critique of Judgment* (*CJ*), one has to acknowledge that the power of imagination is at work in

---

[1] The *Critique of Pure Reason* (*CpR*) is quoted according to the original pagination of the first (A) and the second (B) editions. All other works by Kant are quoted by volume and page number of the "Akademie Ausgabe" (*Kants gesammelte Schriften*. Berlin: Walter de Gruyter, 1902). As a rule I rely on the translations of Kant's text in *The Cambridge Edition of the Works of Immanuel Kant* (Cambridge:Cambridge University Press, 1992), though sometimes there are small deviations that are not marked.

[2] This is meant to be a caricature. Scholarly assessments of the role of imagination in Kant's theoretical philosophy are admittedly more subtle and nuanced. In what follows I address some among numerous publications on the topic. Nevertheless, there is the tendency to understate the function of the power of imagination either by assimilating it too closely to the understanding (see Paul Guyer, *The Deduction of the Categories*. In P. Guyer, ed., *The Cambridge Companion to Kant's Critique of Pure Reason*. Cambridge:Cambridge University Press, 2010, 118-150) or by discrediting it as a relic from an outdated psychological model of mental activities (see Peter Strawson, The Bounds of Sense: An Essay on Kant's *Critique of Pure Reason*. London: Methuen, 1966, 40 ff.). It is worth noting that in a later article, "Imagination and Perception," (In: P.F.Strawson, *Freedom and Resentment and Other Essays*. London: Methuen, 1979, 45-65) Strawson grants the power of imagination a more positive role in the process of establishing cognitive objects.

many seemingly disparate contexts. It can seem as if the only common ground among these different functions of imagination is that it always synthesizes, connects, brings together (*zueinander hinzutun*, cf. *CpR*, A 77/B 103) different items into a unified complex. It is thus tempting to follow Paul Guyer by asking: "[I]s there sufficient reason to accept the assertion of the existence of a transcendental imagination within Kant's theory of the conditions of the possibility of human knowledge?"[3]

This study is an attempt to answer this question. It is a study of how the power of imagination is, according to Kant, supposed to contribute to cognition within his framework for explaining its possibility. It is meant to be an *immanent* and a *reconstructive* endeavor, relying solely on Kant's own resources when he tries to determine what material, faculties, and operations are necessary for cognition of objects. It is immanent in that it presents Kant's considered view on this subject, without questioning this view. But this view must first be reconstructed by retracing some of Kant's basic assumptions and sometimes obscure considerations in order to integrate them into a comprehensible account. This is to say that this study did not originate in a desire to justify or criticize any aspect of Kant's epistemology, only to satisfy the curiosity of a person who (like me) always wanted to know more about the power of imagination in Kant's theoretical philosophy, but was too lazy to spend much time on this topic. Curiosity sometimes gets rewarded, sometimes not. In the case of the power of imagination, it definitely gives rise to thoughts that are otherwise hard to come by.

This study is divided into two sections, each of which contains three subsections. Section 1 deals with Kant's views concerning the

---

[3] Paul Guyer, "Is There a Transcendental Imagination?" In Günter Abel, ed., *Kreativität: XX. Deutscher Kongress für Philosophie, Kolloquienbeiträge.* Hamburg: Felix Meiner, 2006, 462 ff. I want to clarify at the outset that my question is going to differ from the question about whether the imagination is the "common root" (*CpR*, A 15/B 29) of sensibility and understanding, a question posed by the German Idealists and revitalized by Heidegger. As Dieter Henrich demonstrated more than sixty years ago (in his "Über die Einheit der Subjektivität," *Philosophische Rundschau* 5, 3, 1955, 28-69), this question is ill conceived and unworthy of further pursuit.

power of imagination as outlined in the A- and B-editions of the *CpR*. In Section 1.1, I explain why it is so difficult to find a genuine place for the power of imagination within the boundaries of Kant's theory that shows this power to be independent of the understanding. This section is meant to cast doubt on the prospect that the imagination can possess an autonomous function within object constitution, as Kant understands it. Section 1.2 offers a different conception of object constitution, according to which the imagination *must* play a self-standing role. This conception relies heavily on the assumption that Kant wants to distinguish among different stages or phases within the process of object constitution. Section 1.3 gives evidence in favor of my reading by arguing that it helps explain Kant's motivation for rewriting the Transcendental Deduction in the B-edition in the way he does. It also answers some objections against the claims put forward here that are based on textual and terminological grounds.

Section 2 focuses on the power of imagination in the first part of the *CJ*. Section 2.1 examines how Kant establishes the distinction between an aesthetic and a cognitive judgment by clarifying the contribution of the power of imagination to the operations of what Kant here calls "the reflecting power of judgment." I argue that Kant takes the power of imagination to perform an independent activity, irrespective of whether an aesthetic or a cognitive judgment is at issue. Section 2.2 elaborates different scenarios available to Kant for conceiving of a "free play" between the power of imagination and the understanding, both in aesthetic and in cognitive contexts. This section is meant to show that they all comply with his account of the interaction between these two faculties and that they presuppose the independence of the power of imagination from the other faculties. Section 2.3 takes up Kant's cryptic remark that the freedom of the power of imagination consists in its ability to schematize without concept and elaborates its relevance to its independence in cognitive contexts.

This text benefited greatly from detailed and informed comments by colleagues and friends. I am indebted to Dina Emundts, Luigi Filieri, Eckart Förster, Paul Guyer, Johannes Haag, Gary Hatfield, Desmond Hogan, Béatrice Longuenesse, and Sally

Sedgwick for their generous efforts to make the best out of what was (and presumably still is) not always to their liking in the hope of preventing something worse. I am especially indebted to Dina Emundts for organizing a two-day manuscript workshop at the Free University Berlin in 2017 and to Béatrice Longuenesse for her unceasing support of my project in all its many phases. I am grateful to an anonymous reader for helpful suggestions and to the editors of Elements in the Philosophy of Immanuel Kant for including this essay in their series. Very special thanks are due to Andreja Novakovic for her marvelous work, not just in improving this text stylistically but also in eliminating many, if not all, rhetorical super-fluities and repetitions, thereby purging my presentation of awkward obscurities. It goes without saying that whatever still is objectionable and mistaken is my fault exclusively. This Element is dedicated to two eminent Kant scholars and lifelong friends.

## 1 The Power of Imagination in the Two Versions of the First *Critique*

### 1.1 The Power of Imagination and the Understanding

At least three different contexts can be distinguished when it comes to the power of imagination in Kant's theory of cognition as outlined in his first *Critique*. The first (1) is the context of empirical association in which I relate a representation to another on the basis of past experiences. When I hear a barking sound outside my study, I associate this sound on empirical grounds with the representation of a dog. According to Kant and many others, both in the rationalistic and in the empiricist tradition, I am able to bring together the acoustic representation of barking with the pictorial representation of a dog because I possess a faculty of imagination, which in this case works reproductively, in accordance with an empirical regularity or law of association. This context is not at the center of Kant's philosophical attention because he rightly considers the reproductive exercise of the power of imagination to be the object of empirical psychology and he sees no reason to challenge the views of it put forward by empirical psychologists like Tetens and others. Philosophy is, after all, not meant to correct empirical findings.

The other two contexts in which the power of imagination has a crucial function are indeed of philosophical interest to Kant, for they are relevant to the conditions for the possibility of achieving a conceptual organization to what is given through the senses. The first of these two contexts (2) is characterized by the question of how a very specific set of conceptual rules – the categories – can determine a spatiotemporal manifold (based on the affection of the senses and on the reproductive capacities of the power of imagination) to produce a representation of an object about which cognitive claims, i.e. objectively valid judgments, can be made. Kant's answer to this question depends on what he calls the schematizing operation of the power of imagination and is the subject of one of the most obscure chapters in the *CpR*, namely, the eleven pages on the *Schematism of the Pure Concepts of the Understanding*. Context (2) addresses the operations of the power of imagination under a proviso already established in the first book of *The Transcendental Analytic*, "The Analytic of Concepts." This proviso consists, roughly, in the claim that a condition for what can count as a sensory datum, on which schematized conceptual operations resulting in the representation of an object can be performed, is that this datum be amenable to conceptual operations in the first place.

This leads directly to the third context (3) in which Kant wants the power of imagination to play an essential role. Here he is concerned with the problem of how to differentiate within the virtually unlimited totality of sense impressions a sensing subject has at any given moment between those that comply with general conceptual rules and those that happen not to so comply. From a phenomenological perspective, this problem arises from the commonsensical intuition that, among the many sense impressions I have at any given moment, a lot more is given than eventually ends up as the representation of a spatiotemporal object standing in ordered relations to other objects. Kant accommodates this intuition by admitting that it is impossible for a subject to be conscious of *all* her sense impressions at once (A 99). From a more systematic perspective, this problem arises for those who are not prepared to assume that in order for something to be "given," i.e. to be an actual source of affection, it must be conceptually structured. And even if one does believe in this condition, as Hegel does, there is no reason to attribute this belief to Kant. In order to allow for the distinction between conceptually structured and unstructured items *already at the level of sensory input*, Kant enlists the power of imagination and ascribes to it what he calls a "transcendental function" (in the A-edition) or the capacity to give rise to a "transcendental synthesis" (in the B-edition), which is the ability to perform object-constituting actions on what is present via sense impressions in sensibility alone.[4]

I am concerned exclusively with the power of imagination and its role in the third context I mentioned, focusing on questions surrounding the "transcendental function" (e.g., A 123) or the "transcendental actions" (A 102/B 154) of the power of imagination. I focus on this role for two reasons. First, this third context is of special importance to Kant for justifying two of his most basic and possibly conflicting conditions within his theory of cognition: (1) that every nonmathematical cognitive claim that is not analytically true must be seen as the result of a transformative process of nonconceptual content into conceptual form, and (2) that this process must be understood in terms of the achievements of cognitive faculties that are characteristic of a cognizing subject. Given these conditions, the challenge becomes to integrate the basic distinction between the nonconceptual and the conceptual into an account of the distinctive achievements of the cognitive faculties. And I take it that this

---

[4] Cf. A 123 f., B 151. There are many other contexts in which Kant makes use of the power of imagination as a synthesizing activity and in which he attributes to this power specific functions, most prominently in his aesthetic theory and in his theory of schematization. I discuss each of these topics in Section 2, 2.1 and 2.3. I mention these three contexts because it is in these three that the power of imagination plays a role relevant to objective cognition. A recent presentation and discussion of the role of the power of imagination that extends to other areas of Kant's philosophy can be found in Michael L. Thompson, ed., *Imagination in Kant's Critical Philosophy*. Berlin: Walter de Gruyter, 2013. In this volume, the contributions by A. Nuzzo and especially by G. Banham are of particular interest for the topic discussed here.

challenge, specifically in relation to the faculty of the power of imagination, is to be met in the third context. Second, I restrict my attention to the third context because I think that Kant does not succeed in integrating his distinction between the nonconceptual and the conceptual into his faculty-related considerations concerning the power of imagination. This failure becomes most clearly visible once we look more closely at what exactly the power of imagination is meant to achieve and how exactly it is supposed to work in its transcendental function. I also believe that Kant was fully aware of this failure. This is confirmed indirectly in the way he chose to revise the transcendental deduction in the B-edition of the *CpR*.

Before we can turn to the role Kant attributed to the power of imagination in its "transcendental" or cognitive-object-constituting function,[5] it is important to note the puzzling fact that Kant tells at least two different stories, or maybe simply two different versions of the same story, about the contribution that the power of imagination makes to the process of constituting cognitive objects.[6] These stories

[5] As is well known, there are annoyingly many connotations of the term "transcendental" in Kant's writings. But whatever he calls "transcendental" (be it a concept, the unity of self-consciousness, a form of intuition, a condition, etc.) is always (a) given a priori and (b) constitutive for all objects of cognition. Thus I follow Kant (cf. *CpR*, A 56/B 80, also *Über eine Entdeckung, AA* VIII, 194) in taking this connotation to be the term's most basic and uncontroversial meaning.

[6] I use the terms "cognitive object" and "object of cognition" interchangeably. To put this in Kant's own terminology, a cognitive object could be described as the representation of an item that (1) is the result of a conceptual determination of some set of data in accordance with the categories and that (2) can be integrated into a spatiotemporal framework. These two characteristics are essential for a "cognitive object" because it is due to them that such an item can be a referent of a mathematical or empirical concept that can serve as the subject or predicate in a cognitive judgment, namely, an objectively valid judgment about something that fulfills requirements (1) and (2). Thus a cognitive object is an item that is *constituted* by conceptual activities of a cognizing subject whose conceptual operations are performed on a material that (at least in principle) can be given in space and time. This means, as an anonymous reviewer pointed out quite nicely, that cognitive "objects are constituted by constituting their representations." Note that, according to my use of the term "cognitive object," not every item a subject can represent is a cognitive object. Conceptually undetermined intuitions, as well as those products of the power of imagination that do not comply with space-time conditions, do not

or versions are documented, respectively, in the two editions of "The Analytic of Concepts" of the *CpR*. Since Kant famously insists in the "Preface" to the second edition that he altered "absolutely nothing in regard to the propositions or even their grounds of proof" (B XLII), we can expect that he would like us to view these two narratives as different versions of the same story. I thus proceed under this assumption. But this is not the only initial puzzle. What is even more puzzling is that these two versions share the first half. They share most of those statements that comprise the first chapter of "The Analytic of Concepts," entitled "On the Clue to the Discovery of All Pure Concepts of the Understanding." This means they share the third section of the chapter "On the Pure Concepts of the Understanding or Categories." In the second edition, this same section becomes the notorious § 10, which is nearly unanimously believed to contain the "metaphysical deduction" of the categories, to which Kant refers in § 26 of the second edition and which establishes "the origin of the a priori categories in general ... through their complete coincidence with the universal logical functions of thinking" (B 159). At that point the two versions diverge radically in that they proceed to give (under the title "Chapter II. On the Deduction of the Pure Concepts of the Understanding," identical in both editions) completely different accounts of how the categories make the representation of an object of cognition possible. In order to do justice to these peculiarities in the presentation of his view, one has to take care not to get confused by the narrative differences between the two editions in the attempt to understand the cognitive role of the transcendental power of imagination.[7]

---

qualify for the status of a cognitive object. Cf. Kant's explication of what an "object of cognition" is in his letter to M. Herz from May 26, 1789 (*AA* 11, 51 f.).

[7] Oddly enough, the topic "the power of imagination" and its transcendental function is nearly absent in Kant's different attempts to give shorter and less technical summaries of his epistemological doctrines. Neither in the *Prolegomena*, nor in *Über eine Entdeckung*, nor in the prize-essay on the *Fortschritte der Metaphysik* (posthumously published) does he mention the power of imagination as making an essential contribution to cognition.

However, the first task is to provide a short outline of the programmatic framework in which Kant wants to establish his theory of cognition and of the means he takes to be suitable to this task. The most convenient way of doing this is to look at the result he wants to achieve. A familiar way to characterize the gist of Kant's epistemological message is to start with his formulation of the supreme principle upon which all synthetic judgments are founded, more precisely upon which the possibility of the objective validity of a synthetic judgment is founded, and according to which "[e]very object stands under the necessary conditions of the synthetic unity of the manifold of intuition in a possible experience" (A 158/B 197). The claim is that objects *as objects of cognition* – not as objects of thought or imagination, or as a piece of formed matter – depend on the conditions under which they can be experienced. This leads to another formulation of the same principle, stating that "[t]he conditions of the possibility of experience in general are at the same time conditions of the possibility of the objects of experience" (B 197). Because Kant defines experience as empirical cognition (B 147) and thinks of cognition in terms of judgment, this statement can be translated into the claim that an object of cognition, i.e. an object about which an empirical judgment can be made, has to be such that it conforms to the conditions of an empirical judgment.

What are the conditions of an empirical judgment? First, we must note that the phrase "conditions of an empirical judgment" is an abbreviation of the longer formulation "conditions of the objective validity of an empirical judgment." So the question can be reformulated as: what are the conditions of the objective validity of an empirical judgment? Kant's answer is well known. Whatever else might be involved, two conditions are the most basic: (1) there has to be something that is, or at least could be, "given" through the senses and that conforms to the requirements for what counts as an "intuition"; and (2) there have to be concepts that can capture what is "given" as an intuition. These two conditions are, according to Kant, both eminently plausible and utterly uncontroversial because they express an aspect of our ordinary understanding of the term "empirical judgment," that every empirical judgment has to have a nonconceptual object (a "given" object it is *about*) and a conceptual form (connecting concepts in a way that yields a judgment). Assuming that this understanding of what is required for an empirical judgment is correct, which Kant never doubts, it makes sense to follow him in thinking of such a judgment as the result of a process of transforming a nonconceptual content into a conceptual form. If one is inclined to identify the realm of intuitions with the domain of the "nonconceptual," and if one thinks of the "nonconceptual" and the "conceptual" as exhaustive and exclusive alternatives, then the question about the conditions of the objective validity of empirical judgments presupposes that we have already answered a different and prior question about how exactly nonconceptual "stuff" gets transformed into conceptual representations. Kant himself points to this prior question when he declares that the problem one has to solve in any attempt to analyze the conditions of an empirical judgment consists in explaining "how subjective conditions of thinking [i.e., concepts, R. P. H.] should have objective validity, i.e. yield conditions of the possibility of all cognition of objects [i.e., nonconceptually "given" intuitions, R. P. H.]" (A 89 f./B 122; cf. fn. 28).

This link between the nonconceptual "given" and its conceptual organization is provided in the two chapters of the book on "The Analytic of Concepts" (B 90ff.). It is well known that Kant's answer depends on his theory of the cognitive faculties and capacities that have an influence on the formation of an empirical judgment, and that are required if a subject is to qualify as an epistemic subject. It is here that the power of imagination starts to play a role, though unfortunately alongside many other faculties and capacities. Kant's view of these faculties and their related capacities is roughly the following: There is initially the faculty of sensibility, characterized by the capacity to receive sense impressions passively. Next comes the faculty of the power of imagination, whose characteristic feature is the capacity to "apprehend," to collect and connect sense impressions into intuitions. Then we have the faculty of the understanding, endowed with spontaneity revealed in its capacity to synthesize intuitions according to conceptual rules. Last comes the faculty of apperception; it has as its distinguishing mark the capacity to provide unity to what the power of imagination or the understanding (or both) synthesizes according to its rules.[8] This multiplicity of faculties and capacities makes matters confusing and complicated, giving rise to the impression that Kant is exploring different ways of bridging the gap between the nonconceptual and the conceptual. These different ways, documented in the different versions of the transcendental deduction, seem to correspond to different conceptions of what these cognitive faculties are and how they function. Though this impression is not entirely misguided, it fails to explain Kant's systematic motives for involving all of these faculties and capacities in the formation of representations of cognitive objects about which empirical judgments can be made.

These motives become all the more relevant, once we acknowledge that it is far from obvious that all the faculties and capacities Kant lists as operative in empirical judgment formation are indeed necessary for this task. This is especially true of the power of imagination. A prominent passage strongly suggests that Kant can and does establish a link between the nonconceptual and the conceptual without attributing to the power of imagination a role that is distinguishable from what the understanding is said to contribute to this process. The passage I have in mind is what Kant in the second edition refers to as a "metaphysical deduction," though it is an unsolved mystery why Kant chose this name. It is moreover a passage that remains identical in both editions of the *CpR*.[9] In two famous sentences Kant seems to be offering a direct

---

[8] This sketchy outline is the attempt at a summary of what Kant writes about the faculties in B 103ff., A 94, and A 115 f. It abstains from addressing the obvious vagueness and the manifest ambiguities connected with his taxonomy. My sketch, however, diverges from Kant's own presentation in that it distinguishes between faculties and capacities (or abilities) whereas Kant does not draw a sharp distinction between the terms "faculty" [*Vermögen*] and "capacity" [*Fähigkeit*], using these terms interchangeably (see, e.g., A 94).

[9] There has been considerable guesswork for the past 200 years as to why the metaphysical deduction is supposed to be a deduction, what makes it metaphysical, and even where exactly it is located. Kant is of no help, since he does not provide any hint about what he means by these terms. Although there is no

answer to the question of how nonconceptual content can gain conceptual form with the help of two faculties alone: sensibility, which provides the manifold in intuitions, and the understanding, which is responsible for conceptual elements.

These two sentences read:

> The same function that gives unity to the different representations *in a judgment* also gives unity to the mere synthesis of different representations *in an intuition*, which, expressed generally, is called the pure concept of the understanding. The same understanding, therefore, and indeed by means of the very same actions through which it brings the logical form of a judgment into concepts by means of analytical unity, also brings a transcendental content into its representations by means of the synthetic unity of the manifold in intuition in general, on account of which they are called pure concepts of the understanding that pertain to objects a priori. (A 79/B 104 f.)[10]

One plausible way to unravel the meaning of these sentences is to notice that they are based on three general convictions that Kant has already repeatedly stated:

(1) Every empirical knowledge claim (cognition) has the form of a judgment about an object in space and/or time that is, or at least can be, given in some way in or as intuition.

general agreement about the aim and the function of the metaphysical deduction, it is safe to say that nobody would object to Guyer's formulation that "the so-called metaphysical deduction is meant to establish that the categories are the conditions of the *possibility* of cognition of objects" ( Paul Guyer, "The Project of the Transcendental Deduction." In Ralph Schumacher, ed., *Idealismus als Theorie der Repräsentation?* Paderborn: Mentis, 2001, 318. Cf. also Rolf-Peter Horstmann, "The Metaphysical Deduction in Kant's Critique of Pure Reason." *Philosophical Forum* 13, 1981, 32–47.

[10] Though in the sentences immediately preceding this passage Kant explicitly declares the power of imagination to be the source of "synthesis in general" (A 77ff./B 103 f.) and therefore a necessary condition for cognition [*Erkenntnis*], he seems to suggest that synthesis and thus the power of imagination has to bring together a manifold of data according to the rules of the understanding, thereby giving rise to the impression that there is no independent use of the power of imagination in the process of object constitution, i.e. that the power of imagination cannot but synthesize governed by conceptual rules.

(2)  Every intuition as well as every representation of an object has to be thought of as a unity of a manifold of representations that are somehow related to impressions of the senses.

(3)  The unity characteristic of an intuition and of a representation of an object is not to be found in the representations stemming from sense impressions alone.

In light of these convictions, Kant argues in the metaphysical deduction that the unity, which a manifold of representations needs in order to become a representation of an object, is the product of the same activity that is charged with connecting concepts to form (the unity of) a judgment. Because this unity-providing activity is attributed to the understanding, and because the representational manifold on which this activity operates has its roots in sensibility, Kant can be understood as saying that it is the understanding alone that transforms the manifold rooted in nonconceptual sensibility into the conceptual form of a judgment. It thus looks as if Kant wants us to conceive of empirical judgments as the result of a process taking place on two levels. One is the level of the manifold of sensibility, the sensible representations given through sense impressions. On this level, the representations are disconnected, unordered, random, and meaningless occurrences within the general flow of consciousness, dependent on the passivity characteristic of receptivity. At this point, the understanding becomes active and elevates these obscure sensible representations to a level where they are susceptible to manipulation by concepts. At this second level, sensible representations turn into the material on which the understanding performs its operations. It is at this level that the understanding surveys the available material and selects a certain number of the sensible representations in order to form complex unities of representations that are present to the mind as intuitions, namely, as representations of individual objects. These operations of the understanding, which turn a given manifold of sensible representations into intuitions of objects, are not arbitrary acts of spontaneity, but are governed by rules that make it possible to refer to these intuitions by means of concepts in judgments. Kant calls the rules that are the guiding principles of the understanding in producing intuitions out of sensible representations "pure concepts of the understanding" or "categories."

If one is prepared to give some credit to this picture of what the metaphysical deduction wants to convey, it becomes difficult to imagine why the power of imagination would play a role in the process of empirical judgment formation and what this role could be. The faculties of sensibility and understanding alone seem to be both necessary and sufficient for doing the job of providing non-conceptual content in the shape of sensible representations and of transforming this content into conceptual form. However, this would be to disregard that the metaphysical deduction is just a stage in the endeavor to find a "clue to the discovery of all pure concepts of the understanding" (A 66/B 91) – as the title of the first chapter of the *Analytic of Concepts* states – and is not itself the deduction of these concepts. This clue [*Leitfaden*] is guided by the intention of establishing that in order to have objects of cognition, one has to have rules for conceptualizing sensible representations into representations of objects. Because the very idea of an object as a unity of a manifold is, according to Kant, the result of a conceptual operation,[11] and because conceptual operations belong to the domain of the activities of the understanding, the first and foremost task of the "clue" chapter is to show that the understanding has the resources to provide rules that are object-constituting. What has to be shown is that the understanding is in a position to bring "a transcendental content [i.e., the representation of an object] into its representations by means of the synthetic unity of the manifold in intuition in general" (A 79/B 105). Thus in the context of the metaphysical deduction, the main attention is directed toward the claim that there are conceptual conditions for what can count as an object and that these conditions are made available by the understanding. What is of no immediate interest

---

[11] Kant famously defines an object as "that in the concept of which the manifold of a given intuition is united" (B 137).

here are the nonconceptual conditions on the side of receptive sensibility in the process of object constitution. This topic will not become important until the deduction proper. It is quite telling that Kant, when rewriting the deduction of the categories for the second edition, left the metaphysical deduction unchanged. I take it to indicate that what is addressed in the metaphysical deduction is just the conceptual aspect of empirical judgment formation under the intended omission of the nonconceptual basis. And Kant obviously did not see a reason to change his explanation concerning the demands one has to make on the understanding, as the faculty in charge of conceptual affairs, in order for it to be capable of bringing a "transcendental content" (A 79/B 105) into the unity of an intuition. Hence he had no reason to rewrite the metaphysical deduction in the course of drafting the second edition.

Even if one accepts the view that the metaphysical deduction successfully establishes a link between the conceptual and the nonconceptual elements involved in the formation of an empirical judgment by insisting on the necessary contribution of conceptual rules of the understanding in the presentation of objects about which empirical judgments can be made, this success appears to rest on a premise that Kant does not defend either in the metaphysical deduction itself, or elsewhere in the "clue" chapter. This premise concerns the organization of the matter that is unified by the activity of the understanding into representations of objects. In other words, it concerns the manner in which, according to Kant, sensible representations have to be present to the mind in order to count as representations out of which the understanding can form representations of objects. The metaphysical deduction implicitly presupposes that the sensible representations, on which the understanding synthetically operates, are such that they *can* be unified into object representations. This again presupposes that a manifold of sensible representations can be unified into intuitions, because these sensible representations are themselves intuitions. But why and how is this presupposition justified? Why is it that we have to think of sensible representations as something that can be unified into intuitions, and how does it come to be that, if they can be unified in this way, they can lead to representations of objects? These questions have to be taken seriously, not only because they bear on the soundness of the argument of the metaphysical deduction. Kant has to avoid the impression that objects of cognition are based in random collections of sensible representations, which the understanding happens to single out as intuitions in order to unify them according to its rules. He has to avoid this impression, if he does not want to give up on his reasonable claim that it is not enough for an empirical object to be grounded in whatever sensible representations happen to be around, but that there has to be an inherent affinity among those sensible representations that end up as intuitions out of which an object of cognition can be constituted. There must be more to sensible representations than just the fact that they occur in the mind, if they are to qualify as representations out of which "given" intuitions can arise, intuitions that can be united into the representation of an object.[12] This means that Kant has to concentrate more closely on what is happening on the sensibility side of object constitution up to the point where intuitions start to play a role. And this is exactly what Kant is doing by invoking the power of imagination in both versions of the "deduction" chapter, though the first version is much more detailed with respect to the power of imagination than the second and follows a different strategy.

In order to appreciate the problems Kant has to face when it comes to the contribution of sensibility in the formation of cognition, it might be helpful to step back and rehearse his

---

[12] Kant does not have to address these questions concerning the possibility of unifying sensible material into intuitions in order to be able to distinguish between "real" objects like trees, thunderstorms, or redness and "freakish" objects like unicorns, golden mountains, or uncaused events. Since both "freakish" and "real" objects have an intuitive basis in sense impressions and their respective representations, it is not at the level of sensibility, but in the categorial processing of intuitions by the understanding, that things go wrong in the case of "freakish" objects.

views on the connection between the different elements that are at work in bringing about an empirical judgment. I focus on those aspects of this story that shed light on the role of the power of imagination. Let us take as a paradigm case of an empirical judgment "the house in front of me on the other side of the garden has a black roof" and allow that this judgment is based on my perceptual situation. What occurred with and in me in order for me to arrive at this cognitive claim? According to Kant, a genealogical account of this judgment has to acknowledge both subjective and objective conditions of its possibility. The most important among the objective conditions is that there be a "source of affection" (to use Kantian vocabulary), something that *we can interpret at some point in the cognitive process* as an object that causes a sensation. As subjective conditions we have to admit three faculties: sensibility, the power of imagination, and apperception, together with their respective capacities to receive, to apprehend synthetically, and to unify diverse representations into the representation of an object.[13]

Within the framework of these conditions, Kant starts his analysis with a phenomenological assessment of the initial perceptual situation[14] a judging subject is in. In every perceptual situation, there have to be sense impressions or sensations [*Empfindungen*] that the subject receives. These sense impressions are modifications of the sensory system of the subject and as such physiological

---

[13] A 94. It is interesting to note that Kant gives a prominent place to these three faculties as fundamental subjective conditions of cognitions only in the first edition. In fact his theory of the three syntheses, which is so central to the A-version of the *Deduction*, depends on his recourse to exactly these three faculties. Of these Kant says that they "make possible the understanding and by means of it all experience as an empirical product of the understanding" (A 97 f.). Interestingly enough, in the A-Deduction he does not think of the understanding as one of the "original sources ... that contain the conditions of the possibility of all experience" (A 94), which might be the reason that later in the A-Deduction (A 119) he remains a bit unclear especially about the relation of the understanding to the power of imagination.

[14] Though perceptual situations can involve sensory input by each of the five senses, I proceed on the traditional assumption that seeing is best suited for sketching perceptual processes.

states,[15] not modifications of the subject's conscious mental states, and have intrinsically no relation to each other. They are just affections of the senses, an amorphous material, preconsciously present, out of which sensible representations might be formed. In the case of the empirical judgment about the roof of the house, these sensations consist of whatever data stimulate my sense organs, irrespective of whether or not they have something to do with the house and its roof, as long as some among them can yield the representation of a house with a black roof. Sense impressions understood as non-specified content give rise to sensible representations as soon as they become conscious.[16] By "becoming conscious" I take Kant to mean that, whenever I make a sense impression the object of my attention, I thereby create a sensible representation. Kant calls conscious sensible representations

[15] This physiological status of a sensation is somewhat obscured by the fact that Kant uses the terms "sensation" [*Empfindung*] and "impression" [*Eindruck*] both in the first and in the third *Critique* quite often interchangeably (cf., e.g., A1 and B1; A 99; A 120; *AA* 5, 224, and 325; *AA* 7, 176, and 212). Although he nowhere, to my knowledge, explicitly characterizes sensations as physiological states, he does so with respect to impressions (*AA* 7, 176).

[16] This could give rise to the question whether it is necessary or even makes sense to distinguish between sensible representations that are not conscious and conscious sensible representations. It is not discussed here. However, I believe that such a distinction cannot be made within a Kantian framework for the simple reason that representation presupposes an actual representer. See, e.g., the "stepladder" [*Stufenleiter*] of representations in A 320/B 376 f. Against this claim one could object that Kant himself in § 5 of his *Anthropology* (*AA* 7, 135 f.) allows for "representations that we have without being conscious of them," thus apparently confirming the existence of nonconscious representations. However, as his remarks on this topic show, he is addressing as unconsciously present those partial representations [*Teilvorstellungen*] of whatever I consciously represent that I can infer as being contained in the conscious representation at hand. I take him to draw a distinction between what in a conscious representation I am immediately conscious of and what in that very same conscious representation I am only obscurely or tacitly conscious of. Kant here wants to distinguish between different modes of consciousness I can have of a representation, not between representation with and without consciousness. However, note that Kant's stance toward conscious representations is somewhat confusing and leads to substantial terminological problems, especially in the A-edition of the *CpR*. Where this confusion stems from is outlined at the end of Section 3.

"perceptions" (cf. A 120/B 160). Because perceptions are conscious representations, they are subject to the conditions of consciousness, which means that they must be such that one *can* be conscious of them. Because perceptions are sensible representations, they also have to conform to the conditions of sensibility, which means that they represent their content as having some definite position in space and time.[17] Perceptions function as the ultimate building blocks or the basic units out of which intuitions (of as yet undetermined individual objects) are formed. When it comes to their intrinsic characteristics, perceptions have to be thought of as representations of qualitatively distinguishable singular patches of colors and shapes following each other in time. Thus in the example of the house on the other side of the garden with the black roof, the relevant perceptions could be the perception of an angular red patch, followed by a perception of an angular black patch, which in turn is followed by a perception of some green stuff, etc.[18]

[17]  This Kantian view that "raw" or unprocessed sensations have no space and time determinations and that these determinations do not emerge before the level of conscious representations is reached has not been appreciated, either within Kant scholarship (excepting W. Waxman) or within modern sense datum theories. For Kant, it is an essential cornerstone in his defense of the ideality of appearances. Telling formulations of this point can be found in the *Anticipations of Perception*: "Sensation in itself is not an objective representation, and in it neither the intuition of space nor that of time is to be encountered" (B 208); and even as late as in the *Opus postumum*: "Space and time ... are intuitions ... which only belong to us [*uns nur zukommen*] *insofar we feel affected by objects*" [italics R. P. H.] (*AA* 22, 26).

[18]  The clumsiness of this very schematic illustration already points to a problem connected with Kant's atomistic concept of a perception as a sensation of which I am conscious. How are we to individuate such a perception? What belongs to the content of a sensation toward which I direct my attention? The red patch as an item of the perceptual manifold that makes up the representation of the house with the black roof can be individuated only when distinguished from and contrasted with other elements of this manifold. Do these other elements, of which I have to be aware in order to have the perception of a red patch, belong to the content of this perception as well? If so, the perception of a red patch always contains more than just the red patch. If not, this perception seems to have no content at all.

If we take perceptions that are isolated from each other to be the ultimate building blocks of representations of individual objects, we have to introduce, according to Kant, some means for explaining how isolated perceptions can be brought together to produce first intuitions, and then representations of objects. Kant thinks of these means in terms of activities that synthesize and thus achieve unity. The most basic among these activities is due to the faculty of the power of imagination. He holds this faculty responsible for all sorts of connection, irrespective of whether it takes place on the nonconceptual level of sensibility or on the conceptual level of the understanding (A 78/B 103, cf. also A 118/B 164). Thinking of the power of imagination this way leads to the expectation that Kant pictures this faculty as manifested in a uniform procedure operating on two levels and in two stages. According to this picture, the power of imagination, when operating on the sensory level, builds out of a manifold of perceptions intuitions of conceptually undetermined objects. These undetermined objects are called "appearances." On the conceptual level, the manifold aspects of an intuition of an appearance are then processed by the very same procedure into items to which reference via concepts is possible, thus transforming intuitions based on appearances into representations of objects of cognition, to which a subject can relate by means of judgments.[19]

---

[19] This sketch is merely a redescription of what Kant presents in an even sketchier manner in the first two pages of the very beginning of the *Transcendental Aesthetic* (A 19 f./B 33 f.). It is here that one finds the puzzling formulation that has troubled many Kant scholars: "The undetermined object of an empirical intuition is called appearance." As is clear from the above, I take this sentence to say that at the level of sensible intuitions there is no full-fledged object of cognition present, but only its preconceptual sensible manifestation in the form of an appearance, which is an undetermined (intentional) object of an intuition. (There are many different readings around, among them the suggestion already discussed – and dismissed – by H. Vaihinger in his *Commentar zu Kants Kritik der reinen Vernunft*, vol. 2, Stuttgart: Union Deutsche Verlagsgesellschaft, 1892, 30 ff. that the German term "*unbestimmt*" [undetermined] here means "*beliebig*," i.e. whichever object you choose.) A consequence of this reading worth mentioning is that it attributes to Kant an ambiguous use of the term "appearance." Béatrice Longuenesse also hints

What does this uniform procedure of the power of imagination consist in? A short version of Kant's answer could be articulated like this: the procedure that the power of imagination follows in synthesizing "given" elements into objective unities is to gather suitable elements from the sensory level under the guidance of the categories. Let us apply this answer to the example of the house with the black roof. If the patches of color and shape that constitute the perceptual material do indeed qualify as elements of an object of cognition, then I as the cognizing subject must be able to perform the act of bringing together these patches according to certain rules into the unity characteristic of an object. These rules are relevant because not every act of unification of such patches yields the unity of an object. If I bring together the perception of the red patch with the perception of the black patch without being guided by these rules, I could as well end up with a gray patch that, though it could be considered a unity of red and black, is not an objective unity like the representation of the house. Because these rule-governed acts of unification are done by the power of imagination,

at this ambiguity in her *Kant and the Capacity to Judge: Sensibility and Discursivity in the Transcendental Analytic of the Critique of Pure Reason.* Princeton, NJ:Princeton University Press, 2000, 24 f., as does H. Allison in a footnote in *Kant's Transcendental Idealism: An Interpretation and Defense.* Rev. and enl. edn. New Haven, CT: Yale University Press, 2004, 484. On one hand, and most prominently, Kant uses this term in opposition to the term "thing in itself." On the other, he uses it, though much more explicitly in the A- than in the B-edition (cf., e.g., A 101, A 104, A 108 f., A 111, A 119 f., but also, e.g., B 160, B 164 f.), in order to characterize the representational correlate of an intuition, i.e. that which appears in sensibility. Because intuitions are conceived in terms of collections of perceptions and perceptions are taken to be sensations of which I have become conscious, appearances also function as the "object-like" correlates of sensations or the mental representations of the sources of affection. All of this amounts to the view, which I believe Kant to hold, that there are potentially many more intuitions and sensations than there are "real" objects. While the distinction between appearances and things in themselves has attracted enormous attention since Kant first made it, the obscurities connected with the second meaning of "appearance" have not found comparable interest, even though they have, as indicated at the end of Section 3, given rise to considerable problems. For a suggestion for how to avoid these obscurities cf. fn. 44.

it is its responsibility to combine these patches in such a way that their collective behavior fulfills the conditions of "objecthood" [*Objektheit, Objekthaftigkeit*]. These conditions have nothing to do with the intrinsic content of these patches, with redness or blackness or angularity. They demand of the power of imagination to ensure that these patches can be interpreted in terms of category determinations as attributes of a substance, as susceptible to causal processes, and as having the spatial relations they need, if they are to be recognized as constitutive elements of the cognitive object "red house with a black roof."[20]

If one were to delve into the details of such an account, one would encounter a host of familiar problems, mainly with respect to spelling out the exact conditions of "objecthood."[21] These are, however, not its only problems. Especially when it comes to the role the power of imagination is supposed to play, much remains obscure. The first difficulty is why and how Kant wants to distinguish between the power of imagination and the understanding. Kant clearly thinks of

[20] This is how I interpret § 24 of the B-deduction concerning the task of what Kant calls the "transcendental synthesis of the power of imagination" in B 151 f.

[21] These problems are due mainly to difficulties one has to face when trying to get rid of the obscurities connected with Kant's different versions of an argument for the claim that objects of cognition are conceptual constructions. These difficulties emerge particularly clearly with regard to his attempt to connect the unity characteristic of an object with the unity of self-consciousness for the sake of establishing this claim. Yet from a commonsense point of view, the overall line of Kant's thought about how to bridge the gap between the "given" sensations and the eventual representation of a conceptually fixed object becomes plausible on two conditions: if one (1) agrees that there are no good reasons for believing that objects to which we can refer via concepts in judgments are just what is given "out there" in the world all by themselves, but that one should instead (2) think of cognitive objects as the result of a complicated process that has to start from un-interpreted affections of the senses and that involves the active participation of the cognizing subject. Even though nobody nowadays deems it necessary to take refuge in faculties like the power of imagination or activities like synthesizing in order to account for such a process, it is widely acknowledged that the description of the transformation of nonconceptual, sensible content into items that are accessible by conceptual means requires that we endow the cognizing subject with abilities in some way or other. It is an open question whether these abilities are better framed in terms of cognitive or in terms of psychological notions.

the power of imagination as a faculty whose synthesizing activity is constrained by rules – the categories – that eventually reflect the demands imposed by the unity-providing faculty of apperception and that are founded in the necessary unity of apperception, which is the unity of (self-)consciousness.[22] At the same time Kant thinks of the understanding as a faculty that, by exercising a synthetic activity on what is given by sensibility, has to employ the very same categorial rules as the power of imagination does in transforming intuitions into units of reference for concepts, i.e. into objects of cognition. If the power of imagination and the understanding perform the same tasks under the same regulatory constraints on the same material provided by sensibility, why and how are these faculties to be distinguished?

Three options are available for distinguishing between the power of imagination and understanding in the context of cognitive object constitution, if one wants to acknowledge and address the aforementioned suspicion that they might not be distinct. One can deny (1) that these faculties indeed have the same task, or (2) that they share the same categorial constraints, or (3) that they operate on the same sensible material. A fourth option would be to deny any combination of these three. The only option I am going to rule out from the start is the second, since I see no basis for denying that, if the activities of the power of imagination and the understanding are at all governed by categorial rules, these rules are the same for both faculties. Everyone who denies (2) would have to hold that there is a hitherto unheard of list of rules at work in the activities of the power of imagination that cannot be identified either with the categorial rules of the understanding or with their schematized interpretations. This leaves us with options (1) and (3). As for option (1), the claim that the power of imagination and the understanding have to perform different tasks, much depends on the description of these tasks. If one is to focus on Kant's standard description, there is ample evidence

---

[22] Cf., e.g., A 124.

to suggest that he takes both faculties to exercise acts of synthesizing material into unities.[23] Though there might still be disagreement – which has its roots in Maimon, Fichte, and Hegel – about whether they perform their common task in the same way or whether they can be distinguished according to the difference in the unities they are supposed to achieve (sensible unities versus conceptual unities), these considerations do not suffice to burden the mind with two functionally distinct faculties. This makes it highly implausible that the difference between these faculties could lie in their tasks.[24] And option (3), the claim that the power of imagination and the understanding do not operate on the same material, does not fare much better. One would have to deny not only textual evidence from the A- and the B-editions but also some of Kant's basic assumptions concerning the interplay of sensibility and

---

[23] E.g., A77/B 103, A 118 ff., B 135, B 150 ff., B162.

[24] The interesting suggestion by Paul Guyer (*The Deduction of the Categories*) about how to hold fast to the difference of these faculties while at the same time acknowledging the sameness of their task does not really help. According to Guyer, the difference can be conceived in terms of levels of abstraction: the understanding performs its synthesizing acts "in abstraction from the specific character of our sensibility" (144) whereas the power of imagination synthesizes under the conditions characteristic of our sensibility, i.e. it operates on material that is subject to space-time determinations. The distinction of the two faculties through levels of abstraction can be seen as a very sensible and sympathetic appropriation of Kant's description of the difference between the power of imagination and understanding in § 24 of the B-deduction (which is absent from the A-deduction) by introducing two forms of synthesis, i.e. synthesis intellectualis and synthesis speciosa. But does an activity, simply by being exercised on different levels, change into two distinct activities? Is it not the case that the activity of adding into a sum stays the same, irrespective of whether I add apples or numbers? Guyer himself seems unconvinced by his attempt to make sense of a genuine difference between the two faculties within the model he proposes. He explicitly states: "The move from understanding to imagination *is not so much a move from one faculty to another* [italics R. P. H.] as it is a move from an abstract description to a concrete description of our ability to synthesize our intuitions in accordance with the categories" (ibid.). This statement seems to imply that it is definitely not a difference in the task that can be used as a distinguishing mark between the power of imagination and understanding.

understanding, if one were to propose that it is not on what is given in sensibility that both the power of imagination and the understanding perform their actions. All of this suggests that there is no substantial value to the distinction between the power of imagination and the understanding and that, given the dominating power he grants the understanding, Kant would have been better advised to abstain from introducing the power of imagination into the fabric of our cognitive faculties. That Kant himself felt dissatisfied with his account of their difference and their relation is foreshadowed in the A-version of the deduction and becomes explicit in the B-deduction.[25]

[25] Cf. fn. 7. It has often been observed that in the A-deduction Kant already has difficulties in giving an unambiguous description of the relation between the power of imagination and the understanding (e.g., S. Gibbons, *Kant's Theory of Imagination*, Oxford: Oxford University Press, 1994, 18). In the A-deduction one can get the impression that Kant's challenge is the opposite from the one he is facing in the B-deduction: whereas in the B-deduction he cannot find a place for the power of imagination as a faculty distinct from the understanding, because he is focused almost exclusively on the conceptual conditions of cognitive object constitution (which he attributes to the understanding), in the A-deduction he has substantial problems finding a genuine place for the understanding, because he is there concerned with how to cope with object formation under the conditions of sensory input and its processing, which he relates to the power of imagination. In the A-deduction, this leads to the claim that the understanding is nothing but the provider of unity to an otherwise autonomously synthesizing power of imagination (cf. A 119). That the B-deduction tries to devaluate or even blur the distinction between the power of imagination and the understanding can be seen, not only in Kant's efforts to emphasize their similarities (both are called, in B 151, "transcendental," and in the footnote on B 162, we are told that the power of imagination and understanding are only different names for "one and the same spontaneity"). It is also visible in the awkwardness of some of his formulations, for example, when he writes that a certain action of the *understanding* goes by the name of "transcendental synthesis of *the power of imagination* [italics R. P. H.]" (B 153). The contrast between the A- and the B-deductions with respect to the role and status of the power of imagination, as also observed by H. Allison (*Kant's Transcendental Idealism*, 186 f.), figures prominently in Martin Heidegger's attempt (*Kant und das Problem der Metaphysik*, Bonn: Friedrich Cohen, 1929, 153 ff., 201 ff.) to establish that Kant initially thought of the transcendental power of imagination as the original common root of sensibility and understanding.

## 1.2   The Power of Imagination and the Process of Object Constitution

Does this mean that one is better off following Kant's own example after publishing the first edition of the *CpR* and downplaying the role the power of imagination plays in the process of object cognition? Though such a move is quite tempting and likely appealing to many current scholars, it might well carry a price that Kant himself had good reasons not to be prepared to pay. This price is the lack of an explanation of how it can be that on the receptive level of sensibility there is already material fit for the synthesizing activities of the understanding, if no distinct synthesizing faculty, his so-called power of imagination, is involved. If such an explanation is to succeed, then Kant has to assume a difference between the performance attributed to the power of imagination in producing intuitions on one hand, and the actions of this faculty in the formation of representations of objects on the other. In order to see why this is so and to show that Kant was well aware of this problem lurking on the side of the organization of sensible material, one has to revisit and reexamine his analysis of how the representation of an object of cognition comes about.

Earlier I attributed to Kant the view that there are two phenomenologically distinguishable stages on two different levels in the process that leads from sense impressions or sensations to the representation of a full-blown cognitive object, an object about which objectively valid judgments can be made. The first, on the sensory level, proceeds from sense impressions to representations of individual items or undetermined objects, i.e. intuitions; the second, on the conceptual level, proceeds from intuitions to conceptual representations of objects. Both classes of representations, intuitions and representations of objects, are products of some activities of the representing subject.

Given our previous discussion, it is unlikely that the second stage from intuitions to concepts of objects will be of interest to someone who is attempting to secure a self-standing and independent status for the power of imagination within Kant's conception of object constitution. What is going on at this latter stage is definitely dominated by the understanding in that the understanding provides the rules (rooted in the transcendental unity of apperception) without which the necessary unity of an object of cognition would not be possible. At this stage, the power of imagination performs the thankless task of doing whatever is necessary to support the understanding in the endeavor to "bring a transcendental content," as Kant calls it in the metaphysical deduction (A 79/B 104), into a manifold of intuitions, thereby providing the spatiotemporal stability and determinateness to an otherwise unstable conglomerate of perceptions in an intuition. What the second stage is meant to solve is the problem of accounting for the fact that the objects to which we can refer via concepts have to be re-identifiable and numerically identical substances with changing attributes standing in multiple relations to other substances, with characteristics that set them apart from random collections or aggregates of fleeting perceptions. Because there is nothing in the sensible representations themselves that determines their status and their specific connections to other representations (according to Kant and common sense), and because there are conceptual elements involved in the representation of a unitary object (according at least to Kant, maybe not common sense), this determination requires applying the conceptual rules provided by the understanding in its synthetic activity. The understanding achieves this determination by compelling the power of imagination, which is accustomed to dealing with material given in sensibility under space-time conditions, to act synthetically in an object-constituting way by performing a "transcendental action" (A 102/B 154) or fulfilling its "transcendental function" (A 123).

It is interesting to consider what such a view means for the relation between the power of imagination and understanding at this second stage. Does Kant want us to think that the understanding, while engaged in the business of transforming intuitions into representations of objects in a rule-governed manner, merges with or takes over the power of imagination so thoroughly that the power of imagination withdraws and leaves the understanding as the only faculty involved in the transformation process?[26] Or does he want to keep open the possibility that the power of imagination performs genuine synthesizing acts on intuitions that are not subjected to the rules of the understanding and hence do not result in representations of an object?[27]

However that may be, this second stage is based on two assumptions: (1) The synthetic activity of the understanding is restricted to object constitution, which means that the understanding cannot do anything other than combine representations (whether intuitions or concepts) into representations of objects, into representations that are determined by the categorial rules necessary for *thinking* a given manifold as objectively unified or for *taking* a suitable manifold as being united in the representation of an object. (2) The synthetic activity of the power of imagination is not restricted to object constitution, which means that the power of imagination can combine sensible representations into complex representations of as yet undetermined objects, which do not qualify as representations of cognitive objects. These two assumptions, in conjunction with the second stage's explicit goal of providing an account of how exactly cognitive objects become constituted, support the negative assessment that the power of imagination is here of no interest for its own sake, but should be considered only in its service to the understanding.[28]

---

[26] One could interpret some of Kant's formulations, especially in the B-deduction, as pointing in this direction, for example when he claims that actions of the *understanding* can be rightfully described as syntheses of *the power of imagination* (B 153), or when he identifies the power of imagination and the understanding as different names for the same activity (B 162 fn.).

[27] Kant could have been tempted by this option in order to account for dreams, hallucinations, miracles, specters, and other fabrications of the power of imagination "run wild."

[28] This does not mean that the second stage has no relevance for the success of Kant's epistemological enterprise. On the contrary, questions concerning his account of how intuitions become transformed into conceptual representations of objects have been raised ever since the publication of the *CpR*. H. Ginsborg, in *The Normativity of Nature*. Oxford: Oxford University Press, 2015, 55 ff., offers a highly illuminating discussion of the obscurities connected with Kant's view of the constitution of cognitive objects. In recent years, these

The possibility of such a negative assessment might have been Kant's reason for downplaying the power of imagination in contexts in which he is focused on the achievements of the understanding. But, as assumption (2) already indicates, the power of imagination might have more work to accomplish at this second stage of Kant's two-stage scenario, if we start with sense impressions or sensations.

It is nevertheless the first stage, from sense impressions to intuitions, which requires that the power of imagination exercise an activity different from that of the understanding, one not restricted to synthesizing alone. Why is that so? The short answer rests on the difference between the emergence of a representation that has the status of an intuition and the formation of a representation of a cognitive object. This means that not every intuition must be a representation of an object, even when it has representational content. Many Kant scholars might find this view about the difference between intuitions and representations of cognitive objects too extravagant to impute to Kant. As will be seen, such an interpretation relies heavily on material from the A-deduction that plays an only circumstantial role in the B-deduction, if it plays a role there at all. And this fact alone could be a sufficient reason to reject not only the interpretation in question but also the two-stage model I am attributing to Kant, which likewise finds its most explicit support in the A-deduction. I believe, however, that only an interpretation that accommodates the distinction between intuitions and representations of cognitive objects and the two-stage model can make plausible Kant's view that the power of

questions have been discussed in connection with Kant's theory of empirical concept formation and his views about the epistemic status of intuitions, i.e. whether they belong on the nonconceptual or the conceptual side. The latest knowledgeable and thoughtful contributions to these questions of which I am aware are by S. Grüne, *Blinde Anschauung. Die Rolle von Begriffen in Kants Theorie sinnlicher Synthesis*. Frankfurt: Klostermann, 2009, and by K. Vorderobermeier, *Sinnlichkeit und Verstand. Zur transzendentallogischen Entfaltung des Gegenstandsbezugs bei Kant*. Berlin: de Gruyter, 2012. Both books contain extensive references to and helpful discussions of the relevant contemporary secondary literature on these topics.

imagination has a genuine and original function to fulfill – even if it is not obvious why he wants it to perform both non-synthetic and synthetic acts – and can additionally provide a reasonable explanation of the differences between the two versions of the deduction.

But before these contentions can be substantiated, we must examine the first stage from sense impressions or sensations to intuitions. According to Kant, sensations are the initial building blocks of representations of objects. In other words, Kant thinks that the phenomenology of object constitution must begin with sensations (A 19 f./B 34). He takes sensations to be affections of "sensibility" [*Sinnlichkeit*], and because he identifies two kinds of sensibility (outer and inner sense), he distinguishes between affections of the outer and those of the inner sense. Though it is not quite clear how to interpret this distinction,[29] it is clear that he wants sensations to be affections of the organs of the (five) senses and thus to be what we can eventually interpret as physiological events. Sensations as physiological events are "for us nothing" (A 120), as Kant rightly points out, if they are not conscious states of a subject or "connected with consciousness" (ibid.). As conscious states, sensations have a content insofar as they represent qualities like colors, shapes, sounds, etc., and occur sequentially in time (and space). These content-filled representations, which Kant calls "perceptions" (ibid., cf. B 147), comprise the material out of which we form intuitions. And the power of imagination, *not* the understanding, is supposed to be active in this formative process.[30]

---

[29] On one hand, there is an obscurity connected with the conception of self-affection, which Kant himself discusses extensively in §§ 24 and 25 of the B-deduction. On the other, there is an obstacle to making sense of how a synthetic manifold of sensations of inner sense results in an intuition. Sensations that are internal affections of a subject are mostly occurrences of states, not of items that can be turned into representations of objects. I find it difficult to conceive of pain, for instance, as an object consisting of a multiplicity of internal sensations.

[30] In both versions of the deduction, the relation between sensations, perceptions, and intuitions remains somewhat unclear. Sometimes Kant writes as if

Given that there are indeed these three elements – sensation, perception, and intuition – involved in this process and that these elements form a constitutive sequence, according to which sensations enable perceptions and perceptions ground intuitions, this process seems to be divided into two further phases, the first leading from sensations to perceptions, the second from perceptions to intuitions. In which of these phases and in what manner is the power of imagination involved? Is the power of imagination operative in both phases and, if so, in the same or in a different manner? Or is it at work in only one of these phases? I confess that the interpretation I propose is somewhat speculative, since my textual evidence from the *CpR* is rather slim, though some passages in the *Anthropology* hint in the same direction. My intention is to reconstruct aspects of what Kant takes to be the phenomenology of the constitution of intuitions (*not* of cognitive objects!) in order to uncover features unique to the power of imagination.

One might expect that the power of imagination already has a genuine function as a subjective synthesizing faculty in the first very step of this phase, from sensation to perception. After all, there has to be some explanation of how a purely physiological event becomes transformed into a perception, a conscious mental representation with content. This process has to involve an activity of the representing subject, if one wants to avoid either of two hypotheses concerning the essential characteristics of sensations, each of which is rather implausible within the Kantian framework.

an intuition is just a collection of different perceptions, which are in turn conscious sensations (see references just cited). Sometimes it sounds as if he wants perceptions to be the intentional correlate of intuitions only, which would mean that intuitions are the constitutive basis of perceptions, or that they make perceptions possible (B 160, B 164). This ambiguity extends into later parts of the *CpR* as well. Cf. the *Anticipations of Perception*, B 207ff. It also reemerges in the secondary literature, e.g. in P. Kitcher, *Kant's Transcendental Psychology*, New York/Oxford: Oxford University Press, 1990, who is led to claim (in accordance with the A-deduction) both that "[i]ntuitions must themselves be constructed from cognitive states" (113), i.e. perceptions, and that perceptions are "conscious intuitions" (160). Thankfully this ambiguity does not make much of a difference for the reconstruction I offer here (or so I hope).

The first would be that there is no need for a process because bare sensations already have representational content; the second would be that bare sensations are causally efficacious in that they cause perceptions. While the first hypothesis would be hard to reconcile with Kant's conviction that sensations are nonrepresentational in character, the second would contradict the passivity of sensibility. If the transformative process cannot be explained by relying on features of bare sensations – whether they have representational content or whether they are causally efficacious – what remains is recourse to some mental activity of the subject.

So why not think of the power of imagination as doing this job of transforming sensations into perceptions? The power of imagination is after all intimately connected with nonconceptual activities at the level of sensibility and is even said to be "a necessary ingredient of perception itself" (A 120 fn.). This suggestion will admittedly not look promising to someone who thinks of the power of imagination as a faculty whose task consists exclusively in synthesizing individual items into more complex wholes. If the power of imagination was limited to synthesizing, it would be an unlikely candidate for the role of transforming sensations into perception. What seems to be needed here is not a faculty for synthesizing, but rather one for *discerning* – an interpretive faculty that can individuate sensations, which are stipulated as featureless items, by giving them discriminable representational content, thereby elevating sensations to perceptions. Such a faculty would provide qualitatively distinct individual perceptions that "by themselves are encountered dispersed and separate in the mind" (A 120), as Kant puts it. Such a faculty would not be primarily engaged in a connecting activity. And if the exclusive function of the power of imagination is to provide connections, then it would seem unfit for this transformational task from sensation to perception.[31]

---

[31] Unfortunately, Kant himself does not tell us how he would explain the transformation of sensations into perceptions. Maybe he would prefer an

There are two ways to counter this objection. The first is to question whether the power of imagination is indeed restricted to its function of connecting given elements, perceptual or not. The second is to accept that the power of imagination is restricted in this way, but to insist that Kant conceives of synthesis in the case of the power of imagination as a complex activity.[32] This means that it might be preferable to think of the synthesis of the power of imagination as an activity consisting in a sequence of partial acts, each of which contributes to the realization of one synthetic act. This sense of synthesis can be illustrated through an analogy to cooking: in order to cook a meal, one has to perform a series of different activities, such as procuring ingredients, washing them, cutting them up, mixing them, that have to follow a definite sequence. The activity of synthesizing could be similarly described. What it means for the power of imagination to perform an act of synthesis is for it to do different things at once, such as apprehending, reproducing, and connecting. Unfortunately, this second line of defense does not find much support in what Kant has to say about synthesis. He repeatedly emphasizes, in both the A- and the B-editions of the *CpR*, that he takes synthesis to be the act of bringing together, of collecting, of unifying (e.g., A 77ff./B 102ff., A 97, A 101, A 116, B 130). This second strategy is also in tension with the many different tasks that the power of imagination is supposed to perform in many different contexts. Even if one restricts one's attention to the epistemological context, one finds the power of imagination involved in at least three tasks, in apprehending, reproducing, and synthesizing according to rules. Although these tasks are all related to the forming and processing of intuitions, it is not obvious that they are performed by the power

interpretation that relies on the conditions an item has to fulfill in order to become incorporated into the unity of consciousness. One could read his remarks on A 108ff. and A 121 f. as pointing in this direction. In what follows I elaborate how Kant might be thinking about this transition, or, more precisely, how I would proceed, if I were Kant.

[32] Ginsborg, *The Normativity of Nature*, can be read as an advocate of this second way (37).

of imagination through a single synthetic activity, even if it is thought of as a very complex one. Last but not least, though Kant undeniably ascribes the activity of synthesizing to the power of imagination, he does not claim that, if it were not for its synthetic activity, the power of imagination would be idle. On the contrary, he states in no uncertain terms that synthesis is but *one* of the actions of the power of imagination, by explicitly pointing out that the act of running through a manifold [*Durchlaufen der Mannigfaltigkeit*] is distinct from the act of comprehension [*Zusammennehmung*] (A 99).

Thus there is no obstacle to assuming that the power of imagination can go beyond acts of synthesizing, that it can be involved in non-synthetic activities. If the power of imagination can play a role in the transformation of sensations into perceptions, then it does have an autonomous occupation that distinguishes it from the understanding in the process of creating representations of objects based on intuitions, because this occupation is not synthetic. It could also have a genuine function in the domain in which we form intuitions out of perceptions, so in the second phase of the first stage. Since at the second stage the power of imagination exercises a synthetic activity under the influence of the understanding, it is going to be at either phase or both phases of the first stage (so in the transition from sensation to intuition) that the power of imagination can have a genuine function. Because this transition is at least partly the achievement of "apprehension," it is specifically with respect to its apprehending function that the power of imagination can be expected to lead a life of its own, independent of any direct interference from the rules of the understanding.

What, then, is happening on the level of apprehension? The apprehending mind, we are told, "is to bring the manifold of intuition into an image" (A 120). In order to do this it must "antecedently take up the impressions [*Eindrücke*] into its activity, i.e., apprehend them" (ibid.), or it has – to quote another formulation – "first to run through and then to take together" (A 99) a manifold of perceptions. Although Kant understandably conceives of the act of taking up impressions, which I take to be perceptions, as taking place antecedently to the acts of running through them and taking them together, this act cannot be the beginning of the whole process from a sensation to an image. If apprehension starts with perception, there would still be the step from sensation to perception, which would be unaccounted for. How is one to conceive of this step, which is the first phase of the first stage? Or, how do sensations become, in Kant's words, "modifications of the mind in intuition" (A 97)?

It might be helpful to enlist a concrete example. Assume that I accidentally fall into a swimming pool filled with cold and dirty water. What is my sensory situation in that case? I will presumably have millions of sensations or physiological occurrences that result from affections of my five senses. These are purely physiological events, not modifications of the mind, though they are definitely changes in my bodily state. In order to make them modifications of the mind, I have to transform at least some of them into individual episodes of which I am conscious, i.e. into perceptions. As soon as I fall into the pool I become aware of many things, each of which is a disparate item, in rapid succession. I have to notice that there is a feeling of coldness on my skin, that I have the optical impression of darkness, that I have a taste of brackish water, that I hear a muffled sound. How am I to account for this transformation from an all-encompassing, non-individuated, unstructured, physiological event into discrete episodes, thereby making them items that can be "encountered dispersed and separate in the mind" (A 120)? One obvious way to do it would be to introduce an activity that is to accomplish this transition. An activity in Kant's map of the mental is based in a faculty. Because this activity is supposed to be part of the cognitive process, it must be related to one of the cognitive faculties. These faculties are sense, the power of imagination, and apperception (A 94, A 115). Sense by definition is an unsuitable candidate for a transitional activity, because as the faculty of receptivity it can only passively receive data. Apperception is also an unsuitable candidate, because on its own it only provides the form of unity to whatever can be connected.

One might wonder whether the very concept of an individual item that can be distinguished from other items presupposes the possibility of viewing this item as a unit, thus making it dependent on the apperceptive activity in its categorizing function. Though this might be a way to account for the singularity of perceptions, it does not make apperception their material source.[33] Hence, the only candidate left for the transformative activity within the Kantian taxonomy of cognitive faculties is the power of imagination.

Admittedly, there is not much in Kant's texts to suggest that a line of reasoning along these lines is part of his considered view of the transition from physiological states to perceptions of individual sensations that can count as a manifold out of which intuitions are formed. But if we were allowed to attribute such a line of reasoning to him, he would be in the position to kill two birds with one stone. On one hand, he would have gained resources for individuating sense impressions, which present a problem for every causal theory of perception that starts with physiological episodes in the shape of sense impressions as the initial building blocks of perception. On the other, he would be able to provide an argument for the power of imagination as an independent and irreducible faculty, without which cognition would not be possible. Such a position on the power of imagination would imply that its task – at least in its productive function[34] – does not consist solely

---

[33] That apperception in its so-called original [*ursprünglich*] state is not confined to conceptual or categorizing operations, but has the much more basic function of providing numerical identity or "unity in the time-relation of all perceptions" (the term "perceptions" is used here in its first-edition meaning as referring to conscious impressions) is nicely confirmed in a passage from the beginning of the *Analogies of Experience* in the *CpR*: "In the original apperception all this manifold, according to its time relations, is to be unified; because this is what is called forth by its [original apperception's] transcendental unity a priori, under which everything stands that is to belong to my (i.e. my unified [*einigen*]) cognition and thus can become an object for me" (A 177/B 221).

[34] It is unclear whether Kant thinks of the reproductive power of imagination as a capacity that can do anything other than synthesize. He takes it to be a rule-guided synthetic activity (e.g., A 100), but he also wants it to be active in providing representations of objects without their presence (ibid.). The idea of representing something that is not present seems to be in tension with the

in synthesizing items into wholes. Instead, this position would hold the activity of the power of imagination responsible for providing the representational material that, by creating individual and discernible units (perceptions), makes synthesis possible in the first place.

Though a line of reasoning like the one sketched here, whether or not Kant would in fact subscribe to it, might be a way to secure an albeit fragile autonomy for the faculty of the power of imagination against the faculties of sense and apperception, it does not seem sufficient to demonstrate its independence from the understanding. It could well be the case that the power of imagination does the job of transforming physiological states into individual perceptions in a way that involves the rules of the understanding. After all, perceptions are meant to have characteristics that allow them to play the role of a manifold out of which intuitions can be formed that in turn function as the material out of which the understanding produces the representation of an object. Thus, the fact that they are necessary elements in the formation of object representations seems to submit them to the same rules that are operative on the level of intuitions. If I were subject to some hitherto unheard of synesthetic experiences, if my imaginative processing of sensations led to conscious episodes that could not fit together – if I sometimes have an acoustic perception of what for a "normal" person would be a color experience or a tactile perception of smells, whereas at other times my acoustic perceptions contained what others experience as feelings of pressure and my optical perceptions shifted between being experiences of noises and tastes – then these perceptions could not become elements of an intuition. Hence the power of imagination must transform physiological events "in the right way." And would not "the right way" have to be defined in terms of object-constituting synthetic

idea of synthesizing. If I reproduce the representation of thunder after having the representation of lightning, I am following a rule for combining representations that are often connected. But is the act of *generating* the representation of thunder itself a synthetic act?

rules, which would make the power of imagination once again dependent on the understanding?

This objection is unconvincing because it is self-defeating. The very notion of "the right way" makes sense only when contrasted with other ways. And if there are other ways in which the power of imagination can perform the transformational task at hand, this seems to imply its *independence*. To acknowledge that the power of imagination could do differently, could act in such a way that disables the resulting perceptions from entering into an intuition, is to accept that it is a self-standing faculty, relatively free to do whatever it wants. It is not difficult to think of examples of such misdeeds. Think of a sexual episode. In such an episode there are many sensations around that are "accompanied by consciousness," perceptions so diverse that they cannot be unified into an intuition, which could become the basis for the representation of an object. It is not just that in such an episode the perceptions are diverse, but it could even seem as if the power of imagination almost willfully creates them such that they prove resistant against any attempt at unification. Since the power of imagination is able to act in these wayward ways, the fact that it can and does (but does not have to) create perceptions that meet the standards of the understanding indicates, to the contrary, that it is not constrained by its rules. It seems to be up to the power of imagination to "decide" whether to conform to what the understanding needs in order to form representations of objects. The only rule it must obey, as Kant points out quite explicitly (A 99), is the rule of sensibility. It has to let perceptions form a sequence in time.[35]

If one accepts that the power of imagination has "freedom" from the rules of the understanding at the first phase of the first stage, one could naturally wonder whether this "freedom" extends to the second phase of this stage as well, which is the phase from perception to intuition. Recall that both phases of this stage involve

---

[35] Thinking of the (productive) power of imagination as having some degree of "freedom" at this first phase of the first stage opens up a way of connecting Kant's conception of the power of imagination in the first *Critique* to his conception of it in the third *Critique*.

a mental activity, performed by the power of imagination in its capacity to operate exclusively on the level of sensibility, so in a nonconceptual way. The task of this second phase is no longer to arrive at perceptions, but to create intuitions out of perceptions. Kantian intuitions have to be understood as unified collections of perceptual data, of which I am conscious. Therefore the task that the power of imagination has to perform now consists in actively running through [*durchlaufen*] the perceptions at hand in order to select those that qualify for bringing about an intuition of an as yet undetermined object.

How does this selection process work? The power of imagination finds itself confronted with a large number of perceptions, only some of which are such that they can be connected into the unity of an intuition. Thus, to return to phenomenology, in any given situation I will have some sound perceptions, some color and shape perceptions, different smell and taste perceptions, all of them ordered in time without having any reason "to summon to the subsequent [perceptions] a perception from which the mind did move on to another" (A 121). In order to introduce an object-representation-enabling structure into this sequence of heterogeneous perceptions, the power of imagination has to pick out those that are of the right kind because they fit together into the unity of an intuition. If I were (synesthetically) conscious of a colored sound perception, accompanied by a tactile smell perception, and followed by an optical perception of a taste, there would be no way for the power of imagination to make them fit together into an intuition. And even if my perceptions were not as "non-objectifiable" as these synesthetic perceptions, but instead complied with the "normal" sense distribution, it could still be the case that they cannot be combined into a single intuition. Just think of the perception of a color in front of you and the almost simultaneous perception of a sound in the far distance. Actually, the very possibility of becoming conscious of different sensations as individual events depends on the inherent independence of perceptions from intuitions. A perception is in its own right more than just the ingredient of an intuition. In other words, I can have a perception without thereby having an intuition, even if merely an incomplete one. Hence the power of imagination has to seek out the right kind of perceptions, namely, those that can be used in the process of constituting a unitary intuition.

The power of imagination in this selective capacity is guided by a single criterion: whether a perception can be integrated into an intuition, which is a unity compatible with what Kant calls the "objective unity of apperception" (in § 18 of the B-deduction). Kant's phenomenologically plausible idea is that only those collections of perceptions that do not interfere with my being able to think of myself as an identical subject can have the unity of an intuition. If just any collection of perceptions qualified for the status of a unitary intuition, then a similar situation would occur as in the case where no synthetic connection between representations is possible: in such a situation, as Kant rightly points out, "I would have as multicolored, diverse a self as I have representations of which I am conscious" (B 134). This shows that the demand for unity in connection with an intuition is not immediately related to the demand for the unity of an object, based on the category "unity" in the table of categories.[36] That an intuition must possess a specific unity is due to the demands connected with the possibility of a unified and identical self. The unity of an intuition is not owed to an object-constituting concept

---

[36] J. McDowell, *Having the World in View*. Cambridge, MA: Harvard University Press, 2009, also emphasizes that, though the unity of an intuition "is intelligible only in the context of apperceptive spontaneity," this does not "need to be seen as resulting from free cognitive activity" (72, cf. also 96ff.), i.e. from the activity of categorially determining an object in a judgment. I take it that W. Waxman's claim "that there are indeed several noncategorial and nondiscursive ... guises of apperception and that these are presupposed by the categories" ( *Kant's Anatomy of the Intelligent Mind*. Oxford: Oxford University Press, 2014, 5) is meant to point in the same direction: in Kant, there is a conception of unity that is solely due to the demands of apperception, without any involvement of the understanding.

and is therefore not a conceptual ingredient provided by the understanding.[37]

If the power of imagination produces intuitions by uniting perceptions in the manner just sketched, can it be called "free" or "independent" or "autonomous" in the same way as it was in the process of transforming physiological events into perceptions? Obviously not. In the latter case, the power of imagination can be said to be "independent" or "autonomous" because neither apperception nor the rules of the understanding appear to interfere in the transformational process, and it can be said to be "free" because it is free to follow either no rules or rules that are exclusively its own. In the former case, however, the power of imagination is definitely restricted in its activities by the demands of unity imposed by apperception, even if not by the understanding. Although subjection to the conditions under which the unity of the self is possible is without doubt a constraint on the "freedom" of the power of imagination, it is a much less rigorous constraint than the limitations that accompany the understanding. If one were to call the freedom that the power of imagination enjoys in the context of the production of perceptions "absolute" freedom, one can think of its freedom in the process of forming intuitions as "relative" freedom. But even when its freedom is relative, the power of imagination remains completely independent of the operations of the understanding. It is in this sense still autonomous.[38]

---

[37] The distinction between unity as an object-constituting concept (a category) and unity as an achievement and characteristic of apperception is pointed out nicely by Kant in B 131.

[38] In her careful analysis of what she calls the "aesthetic" (purely subjective) conditions of cognition that Kant presents in both editions of the first and in the third *Critique*, F. Hughes (*Kant's Aesthetic Epistemology*. Edinburgh: Edinburgh University Press, 2007) also emphasizes the independence of the operations of the power of imagination from those of the understanding, if the power of imagination is to play the role of a genuine mediating faculty between sensible data and representations of objects. So she grants the power of imagination a kind of freedom (126ff.). But by claiming that "imagination generates a figure that holds together the manifold in intuition *as if* it were about to be unified under a concept and yet the subsumption does not occur"

That there is a difference between being dependent on apperception alone and being dependent on the rules of the understanding is revealed, not just in the different degrees of freedom connected with these dependencies, but also in the results of the activities of the power of imagination. In the process of uniting a manifold of perceptions into an intuition, all that the power of imagination has to achieve is intuitive unity. But when acting in the service of the understanding, the power of imagination has to accomplish objective unity or the unity of an object. Kant makes quite clear – at least in the A-deduction – that there is a fundamental difference between an intuition and the representation of a cognitive object (A 124). An intuition, as a unified collection of perceptions that fit together and can be brought under an apperceptive unity, has to be such that the understanding might be able to use it as material for creating a general representation (i.e., a concept) of an object. Or to put it metaphorically, an intuition has to contain the promise of an object.[39] In order to become the representation of an object, an intuition has to be treatable or manageable by the understanding, which means that it has to be accessible to categorization. This accessibility condition is not fulfilled by a single intuition, but presupposes what Kant calls "a manifold of intuition."[40] Otherwise one would never arrive at

---

(282) she seems to weaken its independence and subject it to the influence of the understanding.

[39] This metaphor is meant to paraphrase Kant's puzzling statement at the beginning of the *Transcendental Aesthetics* that the *undetermined* object of an intuition is called appearance (A 20/B 34).

[40] There is an ambiguity in Kant's use of the term "manifold of intuition," which I suspect he occasionally willfully exploits. On one hand, this term refers unproblematically to the manifold of perceptions out of which a single *intuition* is formed. On the other, it seems to refer also to the manifold aspects that a single *object* can have when given "in intuition." In looking at my jacket in front of me, I have an intuition of that jacket from a certain perspective. Looking at it from another position will give me a different intuition of that jacket. If I call the representation of a single object, of which I can have different views, an "intuition," then the term "manifold of intuition" will refer to the multiple appearances that an object given "in intuition" will have. One would expect me to have two intuitions of one object and not a manifold of intuition,

a general representation of an object of cognition. By insisting on the difference between an intuition and the representation of a cognitive object, Kant does account for a preconception, which has a solid basis in the phenomenology of perception, that many of the intuitions we have do not end up in representations of objects. It is only those intuitions that can give rise to reproductive and recognitional activities that enable a representation of an object. These activities, although they involve the power of imagination *"in its transcendental function"* as well, are subject to the categorial rules of the understanding and start their work on the next, second stage of the long path from sensation to the representation of an object, whose concept can function as a predicate in a judgment. Here in the second stage, which begins with intuitions, conceptual elements in the shape of the categories have their debut, and the power of imagination seems to lose its freedom, independence, and autonomy. Fortunately, Kant does not abandon the power of imagination to this sad fate. As he points out years later in the *Critique of the Power of Judgment,* the power of imagination can sustain a certain freedom even at this stage, visible primarily not in cognitive processes, but in aesthetic contemplation.

### 1.3   Problems with and without Solutions

These somewhat longwinded considerations were motivated by the attempt to find out whether and, if so, where there is room inside the framework of Kant's epistemological model for an independent and autonomous faculty of the power of imagination, whose tasks could not have been accomplished by sense or by the apperceptive understanding. It turns out that there is not only room, but even a *need* for such a self-standing faculty, if Kant indeed holds this specific view outlined here of how the representation of a cognitive object comes about. It turns out that one has to

though the jacket remains the same "in intuition." In this second use, the term "intuition" designates a mode of awareness of an object, in the first a distinct entity.

distinguish between two stages in the rather complex picture of the formation process of object representations, which I believe Kant to favor. The first leads from physiological states or sensations via perceptions to intuitions, the second from intuitions via concepts to representations of objects. I have argued that, whereas the second stage is (due to the necessary employment of the understanding) conceptually infiltrated through and through and thus leaves no room for an independently operating power of imagination, it is at the first stage that the power of imagination *as an independent and autonomous faculty* has to enter and per-form a double role – to transform sensations into perceptions and then to assemble perceptions into intuitions capable of becoming representations of objects. Neither of these tasks can be assumed by the understanding, even less by sense. Thus, I concluded, the power of imagination has not just an independent, but also an indispensable function within the so-called transcendental opera-tions of the mind.

It is worth asking whether one can really attribute to Kant the conception of cognitive object constitution that my reading pre-supposes. As I conceded at the outset, the textual evidence on the basis of which I ascribe the foregoing view to Kant is by no means beyond dispute. One has to be quite imaginative in one's recon-struction in order to find support for the claim that Kant indeed subscribes to such a model of cognitive object constitution, at least "in spirit" (to use a catchphrase from the early days of Kant recep-tion). My suggestions even end up blaming Kant for occasionally accepting terminological inconsistencies and for willfully hiding subtle changes in his position behind well-calculated ambiguities.[41] However, instead of defending my interpretation against potentially recalcitrant textual evidence, I point out

---

[41] As K. Ameriks puts it in the preface to the second edition of his *Kant's Theory of Mind*. Oxford: Oxford University Press, 2000, the reason to take this liberty is "that, even at a fairly late stage in his work, Kant was quite capable of having a very unsettled position on key issues, and that he was especially gifted at deflecting attention from the limitations (in range and in value) of his position" (XIX).

illuminating consequences that such an interpretation enables. These bear mainly on differences between the presentations of his epistemological doctrine in the A- and the B-editions of the *CpR*, as well as on problems connected with terminological shifts in both editions.

The greatest obstacle my interpretation encounters is the fact is that neither the A nor the B version of the *Transcendental Analytic* of the *CpR*, when taken on their own, seem to present this view completely. Rather, it looks as if there is an odd discrepancy between these versions. It is hard to avoid the impression that the A version deals with the first stage (from sensation to intuition) much more explicitly at the expense of a detailed presentation of the second stage (from intuition to concepts of objects). The B version, in contrast, gives an elaborate account of the stage from intuition to concepts, but is quite sketchy when it comes to the question of how we arrive at intuitions. Because Kant offers each version as an exhaustive account of the process of object constitution, one could suspect that there is no single conception underlying both versions. This suspicion naturally leads to the question, widely discussed, as to how to interpret this difference. Has Kant changed his views? If so, why and to what extent? Or is it indeed a difference only in the presentation of the very same position, as he himself alleges (B XXXVII)? If so, how does one account for it in terms of content? It looks as if any choice is inevitably between the Scylla of contradicting Kant's self-assessment and the Charybdis of neglecting obvious discrepancies. Thus it seems best, when discussing Kant's position on topics in epistemology, to stay clear of both sea creatures.

An advantage of my interpretation is that it can avoid this dilemma. It encourages us to think of the second version of the Transcendental Deduction as the result of Kant's efforts to resolve problems that arose in his original first-edition attempt, problems that arise specifically when one saddles an autonomous faculty of the power of imagination with a lot of work in constituting cognitive objects. The following story could be told: while preparing the A-deduction, Kant is quite confident that he can deliver a convincing explanation of cognitive object constitution. This explanation is based on the assumption that it is not just the conceptual ordering by the understanding of a material provided immediately and in the right form by the senses that is to account for the possibility of the representation of an object. Rather, the conceptual side of object constitution is but a second and later stage of a process whose first and earlier stage consists in the transformation of sensations into perceptions and intuitions by nonconceptual means. Thus in the A-deduction Kant advances his theory of the three syntheses, which "give a guidance to three subjective sources of cognition, which make possible *even* [italics, R. P. H.] the understanding" (A 97 f.), emphasizing the function of one of these sources, namely, the power of imagination in its capacity to perform nonconceptual (maybe better, *pre*conceptual) operations on sensible data. But Kant, so the story continues, soon realizes that this account is flawed insofar as does not explain (a) how it comes to be the case that sensations are individuated by the power of imagination in the way they are, as soon as they become "connected with consciousness" (A 120) – in short, how perceptions come about – and (b) why the power of imagination, when under the influence of apperception alone, should succeed in generating intuitions of a special kind, namely, those that happen to be such that they can be subjected to the conceptual activities of the understanding. Both of these flaws are intimately connected to a conception of the power of imagination that credits it with a considerable degree of autonomy, or at least independence from the understanding in the first stage of object constitution at the level of sensibility.

In order to overcome these flaws, two options suggest themselves: Either (1) one uses the activities of the power of imagination to fill the gaps in the formation of intuitions on the level of sensibility that burden the argument. This would mean to embark on the project of disclosing the mystery of how states like sensations, which are utterly nonconceptual, can gain conceptual content. Or (2) one must accept that one cannot find a convincing role for the power of imagination on this level and must choose a different starting point for the endeavor of demonstrating the essentially conceptual nature of a world of objects for us. Though maybe painful, such a concession would not be embarrassing. After all, Kant never had much faith in the power of imagination's transparency and accessibility. On the contrary, on numerous occasions he grudgingly concedes that the power of imagination in its cognitive use stays "a blind, though indispensable function of the soul" (A 78/B 108) whose hidden operations we will unlikely ever find out (A 141/B 180 f.).

Now, the B-deduction creates the impression that Kant chose the second option to overcome the problems connected with his earlier, A-deduction view about the work to be accomplished by the power of imagination on the sensory level. But he realizes this option in a peculiar way. Instead of explicitly abandoning the account presented in the A-deduction of what takes place on the sensory level during the process of producing intuitions and how the power of imagination proves up to this task, in the B-deduction he is apparently determined to overcome the earlier problems by avoiding concrete questions concerning the sensory level, specifically concerning the formation of *intuitions* out of sensations via perceptions. With the exception of a few remarks in §§ 24 and 26, in the second deduction he seems completely uninterested in the sensory level. Rather, there he focuses almost exclusively on the second stage in the process of the formation of representations of *objects*, i.e. the stage that already presupposes the presence of intuitions, on the basis of which concepts arise. His principal aim is to demonstrate that a handful of fundamental conceptual rules (categories) are indispensable to our having representations of cognitive objects at all. In this context the power of imagination and its role in forming intuitions is of interest only insofar as it has a "transcendental" or object-constituting function. If one considers the B-deduction with a view to what it omits in contrast to the A-deduction, one is led to suspect that the later version is a tacit confession of defeat: it documents the abandoned hope of tracing representations of cognitive objects all the way back, right down to their physiological foundations. Fulfilling this hope had required conceding an autonomous role to the power of imagination on the sensible level. This is not to deny that this defeat is compensated by improvements in his presentation of the conceptual aspects of object formation. It simply means that Kant shied away from revisiting what could be called "the first level problems." Thus, Kant is in a certain sense perfectly right to claim, as he does in the preface of the second edition, that he made no substantial changes to either the assertions or the grounds of proof from the first edition to the second. All he did was forgo a topic that has been at the center of the A-deduction, namely, how it comes about that we have *intuitions* in the first place. And he is also right to admit that there are obvious discrepancies between the two versions of the deduction, which are bound to occur with a shift in starting point, but not in goal. As this shows, there need not be a dilemma, since at least the major differences between the two deductions can be accommodated, if one is willing to attribute a two-level approach to Kant. And so what appeared to be an obstacle turns out to provide support for my interpretation.

Unfortunately, this is not the only obstacle one has to overcome in order to dispel doubts as to whether this position can be legitimately ascribed to Kant, if one wants to stay true, not just to the spirit of the *CpR*, but to its letter too. There seems to be a lot one has to swallow, especially in terms of terminology, if one is to believe that my reconstruction corresponds to Kant's texts. I indicate here just three of the most pressing among potential misgivings. I admit that I might not be able to dispel them entirely, since one would have to weigh every single occurrence of the terms in question in order to come to a definite result and this might not prove a rewarding undertaking. This situation is due to an almost vicious lack of terminological clarity on Kant's part, which has the unhappy consequence that one will always find passages that seem to contradict whatever it is one thinks one has discovered about his considered views.[42]

---

[42] It goes without saying that a lack of clarity is not a peculiarity of Kant's texts alone. It seems to be a characteristic shared by almost all influential texts in

What are the main terminological problems that pose difficulties for grounding the reconstruction suggested here in Kant's own texts? The first is the term "perception." One can easily see that there is a confusing shift in Kant's use of this term, not just between the A- and the B-deduction, but within each of the two editions of the *CpR* as well. In the A-deduction the term is used primarily to denote the ultimate building blocks of intuitions, i.e. conscious sensations (A 120, A 225/ B 272). But in the B-deduction it is introduced in order to refer to the empirical consciousness of an intuition (B 160). Instead of thinking of perceptions as isolated elements, of which a multitude are responsible for the constitution of an individual intuition, as the A-deduction recommends, the B-deduction takes perception to be a state of awareness of an intuition and no longer even mentions perceptions as the ultimate constituents of an intuition.[43] Talk about the manifold of perceptions in the first version (A 112) is replaced by talk about the manifold of (B 153), respectively the manifold in (B 160) intuition. But are these observations indeed damaging for the view proposed here? I think the contrary is the case. The shift in the meaning of "perception" can be seen as a consequence – or at least as an indicator – of Kant's reluctance in the B-deduction to address the prominent question of the A-deduction about how we get intuitions out of perceptions, and to start the deduction with given

philosophy. Whether this fact says something about the frame of mind "great philosophers" are in when writing their texts or whether it is rather telling about the nature of philosophy is an interesting question in its own right. People who agree with Whitehead's remark that all of (occidental) philosophy is a footnote to Plato seem to approve the former view, whereas those who complain about philosophy's inability to arrive at unambiguous results might favor the latter perspective. D. Henrich in his *Werke im Werden. Über die Genesis philosophischer Einsichten.* München: C. H. Beck, 2011 explores an original and third viewpoint by focusing on the nature of philosophical insight.

[43] Put in the form of a grammatical distinction, one could say that in the A-deduction Kant can use the term "perception" both in the singular and in the plural, depending on whether he focuses on a single element or multiple elements of an individual intuition, whereas the B-deduction makes the term a *singulare tantum*: it leaves no room for the plural use because it denotes a specific state I am in when becoming conscious of an intuition. See also fn. 30.

intuitions instead. It makes perfectly good sense for Kant, at least within the confines of the deduction, to get rid of a concept of perception that has been designed for a different task and to give the term a different meaning. To repeat, the shift in meaning of "perception" seems to corroborate what has been said so far.

The next terminological worry concerns the concept of "appearance." It seems that this concept already has to have two slightly different – and possibly contradictory – meanings in the A-edition of the *CpR* alone, if the view presented here is correct. On one hand, there is the meaning Kant states right at the beginning of his work when he says that he wants an appearance to be "the undetermined object of an empirical intuition" (A 20/B 34), implying that an appearance is always an appearance of an object of which an intuition is possible or, in other words, that there is no appearance without an intuition. One could reasonably expect that in presenting his basic position, he would employ this term according to this definition. On the other, the impression one gets based on the account outlined here is that he also has a use for the term "appearance" (at least in the A-deduction) that is not restricted to objects of intuitions. According to this use, an appearance is everything that has the potential to function as an item that can be "connected to consciousness" (A 120) and that can thereby serve as a constitutive element of an intuition, even before the representation of an object is at hand. This use points to a meaning of "appearance" that is indeed incompatible with the canonical meaning. One must acknowledge, however, that Kant often uses this term in this second sense, thus giving textual support for the reading suggested here. It is this meaning of the term that allows him to speak of perceptions as appearances (e.g., A 115, A 120ff., A 123) and to claim that not all appearances are cognitive objects (A 124, cf. also A 90/B 123). The situation one has to face is that one has to live with an irreconcilable ambiguity.[44] Although the

---

[44] Kant could have avoided this ambiguity if he had kept to a distinction he explicitly formulates in his dissertation *On the Form and the Principles of the Sensible and Intelligible World* (1770). Here he distinguishes, *already on the sensory level*, between *phaenomena* and *apparentiae* (*AA* 2, 394.). The term

ambiguity in the concept of appearance is confusing and seemingly unavoidable, it can hardly support the suspicion that there is an insufficient textual basis for the account put forward here. Rather, the ambiguity is evidence of Kant's struggle and occasional failure to find a fitting terminological framework for his project.

The third objection based on terminological grounds is the most annoying, for this objection points out, not just an incompatibility, but a downright terminological contradiction the model I have presented has to endure. This concerns the understanding of Kant's concept of sensation [*Empfindung*]. According to my outline of Kant's position, sensations are the "given" raw material from which the entire process of object constitution proceeds. As such, they are purely physiological states that need to enter consciousness in some way in order to become something "for us," in order to have a specific content. As soon as they become something "for us," so as soon as they are "connected with consciousness" (A 120), they are transformed by the power of imagination into perceptions.[45] To think of sensations as the unconscious basis of perceptions seems to confirm, or at least not to contradict, Kant's initial definition of a sensation, according to which it is "the effect of an object on the representing capacity provided we are affected by it" (A 19/B 34). It even seems to fit the claim from the *Anticipations of Perception* that every sensation has a degree of reality, or an intensive magnitude. Yet there is no way to circumvent the dictum in the famous passage containing the "stepladder" of representations on A 320/B 376, in which Kant presents a sensation as a species of perception that is in turn defined as

---

*apparentia* is meant to denote representational material given by the senses *before* it is dealt with by the understanding ("*antecedit usum intellectus logicum*"). The term *phaenomenon* refers to a representation of an *object* of experience, i.e. an item that is already determined by empirical concepts ("*Experientiae conceptus communes dicuntur empirici, et obiecta phaenomena*"). In the A-deduction he seems to have blurred this distinction by using the German term *Erscheinung* indiscriminately for both the Latin terms *apparentia* and *phaenomenon*.

[45] Even as late as in the B-deduction Kant characterizes perceptions as "representations accompanied by sensation" (B 147).

a conscious representation. This ladder seems to turn all of Kant's previous assertions about sensation upside down. How is one supposed to resolve this situation? All that can be done is to accuse Kant of an embarrassing recklessness, probably due to an ad hoc solution to the problem of integrating sensations as mental (and not physiological) states into a taxonomy of representations that has perception – understood as representation with consciousness – as the highest species under the genus of representation. Fortunately, the reconstructive endeavor proposed here is not alone in facing this unpleasant terminological contradiction. The same difficulty plagues any attempt to determine how exactly Kant wants us to conceive of sensation.

So much for the terminological problems connected with the proposal presented here and the hope of overcoming them, which is not that bright. In order not to end this part on a gloomy note, let me highlight what I take to be the positive upshot of ascribing to Kant the model of cognitive object constitution outlined so far. The most interesting point, from a systematic standpoint, is the following: every theory of cognitive object constitution, insofar as it bases object constitution on perception and thinks of perceptions as having semantic content, has to answer the question of how this semantic content comes about. There are many alternatives available, both from the philosophy and the psychology of perception, which connect in rather vague terms the origin of semantic content to brain activities and neuronal processes and thus try to establish a direct link between physiological events (brain activities, neuronal processes) and semantic content.[46] What these theories fail to

---

[46] The most impressive (and extensive) attempt to answer this question of which I am aware is offered by T. Burge, *Origins of Objectivity*. Oxford: Oxford University Press, 2010. I take it that Burge, whose treatment of this question is inspired by what he rightly believes to be a Kantian perspective, would agree that the process of forming a representation of a cognitive object takes place on two levels, the sensory and the representational. However, contrary to what I tried to defend, Burge does not believe that the acceptance of the two-level model leads to a transition problem that Kant in the end cannot solve. This is so because Burge denies that representational activities, of which perception is the most basic, constitute objective content by operating on purely subjective

provide is an account of the conditions that have to obtain in order for an item to have a semantic content. At the least, one expects that such an item can be distinguished from other items and that it has a specific singularity that is such as to allow a one-to-one correspondence between the item and its semantic content. Although Kant might not have convincingly explained how the power of imagination can achieve the distinctiveness and singularity of perceptions through the operations it performs on an otherwise amorphous physiological material, he has at any rate recognized the need to tackle and answer this question. It is primarily the A-version of the deduction that attests to this recognition, for in it Kant explicitly insists on the necessity to distinguish between what occurs on the sensory level in the production of perceptions and intuitions, and what is happening on the level of conceptualization. The fact that in the B-deduction this two-level approach to cognitive object formation stays in the background only goes to show that he might not have been satisfied with his solution, which compels him to saddle the power of imagination with an enormous burden in the act of transforming physiological states into components of particular items (intuitions) on the sensory level in a way that is unconstrained by any rules of the understanding, but nonetheless gives rise to representational

sensory material alone. Instead, he wants us to think of representational activities as resulting from an autochthonous faculty of object-representing that is directly related to a world of real objects. He believes that we grasp the objective representational content in an immediate way. "Thus, primitive objectivity does not depend on individuals producing it. Individuals do not construct objective perception from subjective representation or consciousness. Perceptual representation ... starts with an openness to the physical environment as it is. Perceptual state kinds and perceptual representational content are, from the outset, objective. ... What is distinctive about perceptual capacities is a systematic, structured subindividual, non-agential screening of effects of proximal stimulation for relevance to specific environmental entities" (547 f.). Though such a view would indeed overcome the transition problem, the price one has to pay is rather high. One would have to accept a new (and unheard of) semi-cognitive faculty. Independently of what one thinks of this view, Kant himself would not have been convinced by and attracted to such a bold move.

states with a semantic content. Be that as it may, the systematically interesting lesson to be learned from Kant's approach is that a theory of perception based on sensory input has to account for the distinctiveness and singularity of what psychologists today call "percepts" before it can be of any help to a theory of cognitive object formation.

## 2 The Power of Imagination in the Third *Critique*

### 2.1 Aesthetic versus Cognitive Judgment

From the preceding it seems that Kant, *within the boundaries of his first* Critique, wants us to think of the power of imagination as an indispensable, predominantly synthesizing activity for generating intuitions out of sensations via perceptions, which is the material that the conceptualizing operations of the understanding require, if these operations are to result in representations of objects. On one hand, he sees the former activity as being *at some point* governed by the rules of the understanding. On the other, he is reluctant to restrict the power of imagination, while it is engaged in the transformational task of processing sensations into intuitions, to an activity that can perform its function solely in accordance with the rules of the understanding, i.e. the categories. The differences between the two original editions of the first *Critique* attest to this aporetic stance toward the power of imagination. This stance finds further evidence in the fact (alluded to earlier) that in all his less systematic presentations of his theory of knowledge formation, Kant downplays the role that the power of imagination has to play. This fact generates the impression that Kant is not eager to reengage questions concerning the workings of this particular faculty.

But, as everyone at least superficially familiar with Kant's third *Critique*, the *Critique of the Power of Judgment* (1790), will recognize, this impression is misleading. Here, in the context of an analysis of the conditions under which the aesthetic predicate "beautiful" can be applied to an object, we rediscover him intensely engaged with the power of imagination and the way it contributes to the constitution of an object of cognition. The connection between aesthetics and cognition, though at first sight strange, becomes less surprising if one calls to mind Kant's conviction that an aesthetic judgment is a pseudo-cognitive judgment.[47] Such a judgment is established by the very same activities and the very same faculties that participate in the formation of an objectively valid judgment in the context of cognition. However, whereas a full-blown cognitive judgment aims to determine an object, an aesthetic judgment is directed at an object without aiming at the determination of it. Because of the close relationship Kant sees between an aesthetic and a cognitive judgment, he tries to approach the peculiarities of an aesthetic judgment by looking at the differences between the roles the activities and faculties involved have to play in generating each of them. This endeavor leads him in the third *Critique* to many interesting and highly influential claims regarding the conditions under which an aesthetic judgment is possible. The most distinctive among these claims might be that the possibility of an aesthetic judgment requires a special interaction between the power of imagination and the understanding, an interaction Kant calls a "free play" between them. In this way he makes the power of imagination an important element in his aesthetic considerations.

Though Kant's aesthetic theory undoubtedly deserves the vast attention it has received, it is of interest to us only to the extent to which it can help us get closer to his views about the operations of the power of imagination *in the process of cognition*. This means that we have to find out what he wants this power to achieve in the third *Critique*, as far as it is part of a judgmental practice that is not directly aiming at cognition but at aesthetic evaluation, and how this achievement sheds light on the cognitive use of the power of imagination. In other, more familiar words, we have to relate the

---

[47] There is an ongoing dispute about the status of aesthetic judgments. For a lucid presentation of the main positions in this discussion, see Paul Guyer, *Harmony of the Faculties Revisited*, in *Values of Beauty*. Cambridge: Cambridge University Press, 2005.

theory of aesthetic judgment formation presented in the third *Critique* to the theory of cognitive judgment formation presented in the first *Critique.*[48]

In the first *Critique* Kant discusses the power of imagination mainly under the epistemological perspective of the contribution it makes to the representation of objects. As we have seen, there the power of imagination has to generate intuitions or representations of individual objects (A 32/B 47), to which the understanding can apply concepts (or general representations) in the endeavor of making them cognitively accessible by means of judgments. Concepts – which Kant thinks of as rules – provided by the understanding are necessary in order to have the means of relating to intuitions in such a way that they can be addressed by and determined in a cognitive judgment. Without concepts there would be no judgments, and without judgments there would be no cognition. Thus, concepts are the necessary means for elevating representations of individual items, i.e. intuitions, to the level of cognition. In the first *Critique* Kant thinks of this elevating process in terms of a procedure of bringing intuitions under concepts or of subsuming individual representations under general representations. In his terminology, concepts as general representations are the tools, under which intuitions as singular representations have to be brought or subsumed, in order to make cognition possible. Kant attributes this activity of bringing under or subsuming in general to the faculty of the power of judgment, since it is "the faculty ... of determining [*unterscheiden*] whether something stands under a given rule [a concept, R. P. H.] ... or not" (A 132/B 171).

In the first *Critique* Kant is mainly interested in pointing out how concepts and intuitions – which are intrinsically different, since the former are the products of the understanding whereas the latter are achievements of the power of imagination based on sensibility – must be conceived, if a process of subsumption is to take place

---

[48] This has been done quite often in recent years. See, for example, the books already mentioned by S. Gibbons, H. Ginsborg, and F. Hughes.

between them. This leads him to his rather obscure theory of schematization, according to which transcendental categories and empirical concepts are in need of schemata before the power of judgment can use them in order to determine conceptually the sensible material given in an intuition. A schema, whether of a transcendental or an empirical concept, is meant to be "the phenomenon or the sensible concept of an object" (A 146/B 186), though it might be better called a "sensualized concept" [*versinnlichter Begriff*]. Kant thinks of it as a product of the power of imagination that "realizes the understanding" (A 147/B 187), that gives objective significance to otherwise meaningless conceptual rules. A schema is a "mediating representation" between the purely conceptual (the "intellectual") and the "sensible" (cf. A 138/B 177). The upshot of this theory of schematization is the claim that the power of judgment can perform its subsuming task only if schematized concepts are available. In the first *Critique* Kant provides only a sketchy explanation of what is involved in the process of schematization of different types of concepts (transcendental and empirical), and in the chapter on the principles of the pure understanding he offers a relatively extensive account of how the power of judgment relates schematized transcendental concepts (categories) to sensibly given material. Nevertheless, he remains in the first *Critique* by and large silent concerning the following question: how does the power of judgment function with respect to empirical concepts, and which role is the power of imagination supposed to play?

Though Kant never abandons this view concerning the conditions that have to be realized if the power of judgment is to fulfill its determining function, in the third *Critique* he refines the analysis of what this faculty is supposed to do by looking more closely at the actual procedures the power of judgment carries out in relating the conceptual to the sensible in the case of empirical concepts. The official reason he gives for this renewed interest in the workings of the power of judgment is his renowned discovery of a new transcendental principle, the principle of purposiveness, which he declares to be an a priori principle governing the operations of the power of judgment. Because Kant does not believe the power of judgment to be in need of a priori principles of its own in order to determine a concept by means of a fitting intuition (EE V, *AA* 20, 211 f.), purposiveness can only be a principle of the power of judgment in its non-determining function, if it is to be a transcendental principle at all. Kant calls this new function its "reflecting" function. He thus comes to distinguish between the reflecting and the determining use of the power of judgment, and to claim that only the activities of the reflecting power of judgment are subject to the transcendental principle of purposiveness.

But even before Kant becomes concerned with finding a place for purposiveness as a genuine transcendental principle within the unstable and fragile fabric of the faculties of cognition (power of imagination, understanding, power of judgment, reason), the distinction between a determining and a reflecting use of the power of judgment already has a basis in his conception of the task that the power of judgment is to accomplish. Because Kant conceives of the power of judgment as a relating or mediating capacity that allows us "to think the particular as contained under the general" (E IV, *AA* 5, 179) he has to distinguish between two different cases in which the power of judgment carries out its operations, and thus between two different functions of this faculty. Here is how Kant describes these differences: "If the general (the rule, the principle, the law) is given, then the power of judgment which subsumes the particular under it [the general, R. P. H.] ... is determining. If, however, only the particular is given, to which it must find the general, then the power of judgment is merely reflecting" (ibid.). Based on this characterization, in the third *Critique* Kant turns to the reflecting use of the power of judgment in order to establish his theory of aesthetic judgment. According to this theory, an object is judged to be beautiful just in case the judging subject, without having a concept under which to subsume the intuition of that object, can feel *in the act of trying to find a concept that fits this intuition* (in the act of reflecting about it) a certain "reciprocal harmony [*wechselseitige Zusammenstimmung*]" (§ 9, *AA* 5, 219) between the activities of those cognitive faculties that are necessarily involved in creating concepts and intuitions – in other words, between the understanding and the power of imagination. Fortunately, we do not have to concern ourselves with the question of whether Kant's analysis of the reciprocal harmony of the cognitive powers as a condition of an aesthetic judgment is convincing. A painstaking discussion of every aspect of the details of his analysis has been under way for more than 200 years, without leading to any unanimous results.[49] Nor do we have to take up the question of how Kant conceives of the reciprocal harmony of the cognitive powers, and how this harmony comes about, even though it is primarily in connection with his views regarding this harmony that the power of imagination makes its reappearance as a cognitive faculty in the third *Critique*. Our main question will be: what and by which procedures does the power of imagination contribute to the formation of what can become a cognition? After all, the only reason we have for dealing with Kant's third *Critique* is to find out whether it provides some clues concerning how he envisioned the work of the power of imagination in the process of cognitive object constitution as it is presented in the first *Critique*.

There are several ways in which Kant characterizes what the power of imagination is supposed to do in the cognitive process. These all point in the same direction. Already in the unpublished *First Introduction*, when mentioning the acts necessary to form empirical concepts, Kant writes:

> To every empirical concept belong . . . three actions of the self-active [*selbsttätigen*] faculty of cognition: 1. the apprehension (apprehensio) of the manifold of the intuition, 2. the comprehension, i.e. the synthetic unity of the consciousness of this manifold in the concept

---

[49] See, e.g., H. Allison, Kant's Theory of Taste. Cambridge: Cambridge University Press, 2001; P. Guyer, *Kant and the Claims of Taste*. Cambridge, MA: Harvard University Press, 1979; J. Kulenkampff, *Kants Logik des ästhetischen Urteils*. 2. erw. Aufl., Frankfurt a.M.: Klostermann, 1994 – a very helpful survey of the more recent literature can be found in the bibliography of H. Ginsborg, *Kant's Aesthetics and Teleology*. In *The Stanford Encyclopedia of Philosophy* (fall 2014 edition).

of an object (apperceptio comprehensiva), 3. the exhibition (exhi-
bitio) of the object that corresponds to this concept in the intuition.
To the first action power of imagination, to the second understanding, to the third power of judgment is required. (EE VII, *AA* 20, 220)

In this passage, which details the process of empirical concept
formation, the power of imagination is credited with being in
charge of apprehending the sensible material, the manifold,
which is contained in a given intuition of an object. This characterization, however, appears to be puzzling, if it is meant as
a comprehensive description of what the power of imagination
contributes to cognition of objects and not just to empirical concept formation. Though apprehending might be the main task of
the power of imagination *in the process of empirical concept formation*, it cannot be its only task when considered independently of
this process. A condition for accomplishing the task of apprehending seems to be that not only the manifold, but above all an
intuition containing this manifold be given. In order to assemble
this manifold into one intuition, there should be another collecting
function conceivable that is distinct from the comprehending
activity of the understanding and thus has to be attributed to the
power of imagination. This is so because, as Kant writes in both the
first and the third *Critiques*, the understanding and the power of
imagination are the sole faculties involved in the organization of
sensible material into objective representations, while the power of
judgment has the laborious chore of relating or mediating between
these two. If this collecting function is to be indeed distinguished
from the comprehension done by the understanding, it seems that
the power of imagination must have, not just an apprehending
function, but in addition the ability to form out of the sensible
manifold an intuition that is not yet an intuition of an object. One
would otherwise be committed to the claim that every intuition,
*due to the fact that it contains a manifold*, is subject to the comprehending activity of the understanding, which in turn would
imply that there would be no intuition without a concept or that
every intuition, in virtue of being an intuition, would exemplify

a concept. It is obvious that Kant cannot possibly endorse such a claim. If he did, his first *Critique* notion of blind (in the sense of concept-less) intuitions, as well as his third *Critique* talk of intuitions without concepts, would make no sense anymore.[50]

That Kant regards the power of imagination as not restricted to the task of apprehending alone is confirmed by his description of what the power of imagination is doing in § 26 of the *Critique of the Power of Judgment*. In the context of a discussion of its limitations with respect to the apprehension and comprehension of infinite magnitudes [*Größen*], he again attributes to the power of imagination the action of apprehending a manifold. Somewhat unexpectedly in light of the passage cited earlier, he also assigns to it an action of *comprehending* this manifold, which he characterizes as "comprehensio aesthetica" (*AA* 5, 251). This aesthetic comprehension is obviously not to be identified with that comprehension that is conveyed by the synthetic unity of consciousness to a given intuitive manifold in a concept (apperceptio comprehensiva), because aesthetic comprehension is an act that Kant explicitly attributes to the power of imagination and not to the understanding. In what could the difference between these two types of comprehension consist? Here is one suggestion: whereas apperceptive comprehension is a necessary step in arriving at concepts and involves an activity of the understanding, which performs its comprehending task on already given intuitions, the aesthetic comprehension of the power of imagination is such that it first leads to intuitions that can then serve as the basis for concept formation. And Kant indeed speaks of aesthetic comprehension

---

[50] A blind intuition is not meant to be no intuition, but rather an intuition (representation of an individual item, a particular) that is deficient from a cognitive point of view in that it is devoid of all conceptual content. Kant attributes an analogous defect to what he calls "empty concepts." These too are definitely concepts (general representations), though without any intuitive content. Kant expresses this view quite often, especially clearly in his *Prize-Essay on the Progress of Metaphysics*: "By means of a mere intuition without concept, an object, though given, is not thought, by means of a concept without corresponding intuition it [the object, R. P. H.] is thought, though none is given" (*AA* 20, 325).

as "comprehension into an *intuition* (emphasis R. P. H.) of the power of imagination" only a couple of pages after introducing comprehensio aesthetica (*AA* 5, 254). A remark from the first of the so-called Kiesewetter Aufsätze goes in the same direction: "Apprehension of the power of imagination, *apprehensio aesthetica*. Comprehension of it, *comprehensio aesthetica* (aesthetic comprehension), I bring together the manifold in a whole representation and so it achieves a specific [*gewisse*] form" (L Bl Kiesewetter 1, *AA* 18, 320).

The idea that the power of imagination is a faculty that is responsible for the constitution of conceptually indeterminate intuitions, on the basis of which concepts of determinate objects can be formed, is most clearly expressed in § 35. There Kant discusses the power of judgment as the subjective condition of judging in general: "Used in regard to a representation through which an object is given it [the power of judgment, R. P. H.] requires the correspondence [*Zusammenstimmung*] of two powers of representation: i.e. of the power of imagination (for the intuition and the composition [*Zusammensetzung*] of its manifold) and of the understanding (for the concept of the representation of the unity of this composition" (*AA* 5, 287). Kant once again links the contribution of the power of imagination to the formation of the representation of an object, about which a judgment – irrespective of whether it is a cognitive or an aesthetic judgment – is possible, to the power of imagination's ability to establish an intuition that on its own is not conceptually determined.

The claim that the power of imagination provides intuitions is prima facie fully consistent with what Kant has outlined in the first *Critique* (in both editions). This raises the question of whether the third *Critique* adds anything to our understanding of the operations of the power of imagination leading to intuitions. One notable difference is that, whereas in the first *Critique* Kant seems to be mainly interested in intuitions insofar as they give rise to representations of objects that are determined by a concept, in the third *Critique* he considers them from a different point of view. Here his attention is not directed at those intuitions that result in the representation of an *object* and hence already conforms in some way to the demands of the understanding. While focusing on a situation in which the power of judgment is involved as a mediating faculty between the power of imagination and the understanding, he steps back and turns to the contribution of the power of imagination to the process of establishing those intuitions on which the power of judgment can operate *before* they become the material of the conceptualizing (determining) activities of the understanding.

Given our previous discussion, one cannot help but get the impression that in the third *Critique* Kant is again taking up the two-stage model of cognitive object constitution he seems to favor (though not explicitly execute) in the Transcendental Deduction of the first edition of the first *Critique*. According to this model, a cognitive object – an object whose concept can function either as a predicate in a judgment of the form 'X is A' or as a subject in a judgment of the form 'A is X' – arises through two operations of the mind. There has to be in stage (1) an activity that synthesizes a manifold of sensible impressions into an intuitive whole. This activity is attributed to the power of imagination and its exercise is free from any conceptual constraints of the understanding. When engaged in this activity, the power of imagination may be bound by rules that are specific to its synthesizing operations. These rules are, however, genuinely distinct from those of the understanding in that they do not provide means through which the sensibly given manifold of an intuition can be synthesized according to concepts (like substance, being qualitatively and quantitatively determined, etc.) in order to think of the intuition in terms of an objective unity that is the result of a conceptual synthesis. Then in stage (2) the understanding comes into play as a faculty of synthesizing according to conceptual rules, taking up intuition as the result of the activity of the power of imagination. Only if this intuition is such that it can be subjected to the understanding's synthesizing rules and fit into a schema, which is a rule that the power of imagination provides to the understanding for the subsuming use of the power of judgment, can this intuition result in a representation of a determinate object. In this context, the power of imagination is governed by the demands of the understanding, for it must generate schemata that allow the understanding to relate concepts to intuitions.

This is where Kant's analysis in the first *Critique* of what the power of imagination and the understanding contribute to the formation of a cognitive object ends. But if he is indeed committed to the two-stage model of object formation and thus to the view that the power of imagination is free (in both the absolute and the relative sense distinguished earlier) to bring together a manifold into an intuition in this first stage without interference from the understanding, then he must also endorse a claim for which he opens up space by allowing for blind intuitions, even if he never makes it explicitly in the first *Critique*. This is the claim that there might be intuitions that *cannot* be conceptualized. In other words, his first *Critique* view of how the process of object formation works commits him to take the following for granted: if the manifold synthesized by the power of imagination into an intuition turns out to be recalcitrant to conceptual synthesis, and the understanding finds no way to synthesize this manifold according to its rules, then what remains is just the representation of an individual item, an intuition for which no concept is available and hence no determinate object conceivable. Such a view, however, requires that one grant the power of imagination freedom and independence from the understanding in the production of intuitions.

There is, as far as I can see, no indication that Kant changed his position in the third *Critique* about what the power of imagination does independently from the understanding. He still assumes that the power of imagination acts freely in its passage from impressions [*Eindrücke*] to intuitions, as corroborated by his remarks about aesthetic comprehension mentioned earlier. And there is no need for any change because his stance as to how intuitions are generated stays the same from the first to the third *Critique*. This cannot be said with respect to his views concerning the second stage of cognitive object formation, the stage at which representations of cognitive objects are formed out of intuitions. As we have seen, Kant's idea in the first *Critique* seems to be that it is solely the task of the understanding to select intuitions that are suitable for its synthesizing activities and transform them into conceptual representations. Intuitions are just the material provided by the power of imagination in the service of the understanding, and they lead to conceptual representations just in case the understanding can deal with these intuitions in such a way that what is contained in them can be determined according to its categorial rules. If this determination is possible, then the intuition at issue is one that can be subsumed under a concept. This act of subsumption is done by the power of judgment in its determining use. The question about the freedom of the power of imagination does not come up in this scenario, because it has no self-standing productive function to actively collect a manifold of sensible data into the unity of an intuition. Instead it must be subservient to demands set by the requirements internal to the understanding, if the understanding is to fulfill its object-determining task. In other words, the power of imagination must provide sensualizations [*Versinnlichungen*] of concepts in the guise of schemata.

## 2.2   The Free Play between the Power of Imagination and the Understanding

The third *Critique* can be read as elaborating this picture by providing an account of the distinctive achievement of the power of imagination when viewed as operating independently from the understanding *while at the same time related to it through the power of judgment*. The most important point to note is the fact that in the third *Critique* a distinctive activity is attributed to the power of imagination, namely, to provide an intuition by putting together [*zusammensetzen*] a manifold of sensible data without the involvement of the understanding (cf. *AA* 5, 217, 287), even though this activity takes place in a context defined by the boundaries that the understanding sets for the power of judgment. This already confirms that Kant does not think of the power of imagination, even if related to the understanding via the power of judgment, as operating necessarily under the spell of the understanding, and it already settles some of the issues discussed in the preceding sections about his views on this topic in the first *Critique*. That Kant unambiguously conceives of the power of imagination as independent in its synthesizing activities when it comes to a manifold of data is also confirmed by his talk about the "free play of the faculties of cognition" (*AA* 5, 217), which refers to the power of imagination and the understanding. These faculties are independent of each other and thus free in the sense that each of them can be active and provide specific representations, intuitions, and concepts respectively, without being in need of any support by the other, even if the result of these actions performed by each in isolation will never amount to the representation of an object of cognition, but remain a blind intuition or an empty concept. Their independence is the reason that the power of imagination and the understanding can enter into a relation that can be described as a free play, which Kant takes to be a condition for aesthetic experience. This free play of the faculties, however, does not mean that each of them is free to do whatever it wants. Kant makes it abundantly clear that they perform their actions within specific constraints. The understanding is bound by synthesizing rules that have the status of laws, accounting for its lawfulness [*Verstandesgesetzmäßigkeit, AA* 5, 241]. The power of imagination is restricted in its synthesizing activities to apprehend and comprehend [*zusammenfassen*] whatever is given to it into a "whole of an intuition" [*ein Ganzes der Anschauung, AA* 5, 257].[51]

---

[51] J. Kneller in her *Kant and the Power of Imagination* (Cambridge: Cambridge University Press, 2007) traces Kant's use of the term "free play" back to Lessing's *Laokoon* (41) and investigates in an informative way the role of the idea of the free play of imagination within the context of the aesthetic discussions in the period from Lessing to Schiller (38-59). But her subsequent analysis of what the free play of the power of imagination consists in is to a certain extent tainted by her belief that "[f]or Kant . . . all acts of synthesis are acts of the understanding" (100). This belief is at odds with what Kant writes in *CpR* A 78/B 103 and requires that one rely solely on what he says in B 130, without taking into account the ramifications of this passage in § 24 of the B-deduction that introduces a synthesis of the power of imagination.

Given these constraints, and given the fact that Kant takes an interaction between the two faculties to be necessary not just for an aesthetic, but also for a cognitive appraisal [*Beurteilung*] of an object, it is worth asking how he conceives of the difference between their interaction in the case of an aesthetic and a cognitive appraisal of an object. This question also opens up a discussion of his detailed conception of the free play of the faculties and of his implicit views about the way the power of imagination works in cognitive contexts.

As far as the interaction of the faculties is concerned, Kant's view seems to be guided by the observation that two cases have to be distinguished in a perceptual situation that aims at appraising the representation of an object in terms of what it is. The first is the situation where the representation is a concept, but a subject does not know whether an intuition is available that fits this concept. Let us call this situation "the determinative scenario." The second situation obtains in case the subject has a *nonconceptual* representation, an intuition of something or other, and ponders whether this intuitive representation can give rise to a concept under which it can be subsumed. Let us call this situation "the reflective scenario." Kant apparently thinks of the determinative and the reflective scenario as two distinct situations and wants to integrate both of them into his general view of the interaction between the power of imagination and the understanding in appraising the representation of an object, namely, of something in whose concept a manifold of a given intuition is united (cf. *CpR*, B 137).

It might be tempting to correlate each of these scenarios with one of the two ways of appraising objects that Kant wants to distinguish in the third *Critique*, which means to think of the determinative scenario as exemplifying a cognitive approach to object appraisal and of the reflective scenario as representing an aesthetic approach. This, however, cannot be correct, since Kant explicitly allows for a cognitive as well as an aesthetic assessment of an object in both cases. For him it is perfectly acceptable to judge [*urteilen*], while having the conceptual representation "tree" present in the mind, that the tree has leaves (a cognitive assessment) as well as that the tree is beautiful (an aesthetic claim).[52] He also seems to think that while having an intuition as a conceptually undetermined representation present in the mind, this intuition can lead both to a cognitive and to an aesthetic object appraisal, both to the cognitive judgment "this something here is a tree" and the aesthetic judgment "this something here is beautiful."[53] Because in each of these four cases an interaction between the power of imagination and the understanding takes place, and because this interaction is meant to lead to either a cognitive or an aesthetic response to the representation at hand, there has to be a difference in the way this interaction is realized. As we will see, it is only in the aesthetic cases that a "free play of the faculties of cognition" (§ 9) takes place. I discuss these different scenarios in turn in what follows.

That the determinative scenario of the basic perceptual situation addresses a cognitive situation, insofar as it conceives of the perceiving subject as already possessing a concept that is meant to determine the given representation, is obvious from what Kant points out most clearly in § 9 of the third *Critique* (*AA* 5, 216ff.). In such a cognitive situation I as the perceiving subject have the conceptual representation "tree" in mind. This conceptual representation has the status of a general concept and is made available by the synthesizing activities of the understanding, which is in this case a synthesis of marks in a concept. In order to think of this representation as having an objective content, as being such that an intuitively given item can be subsumed under it, I have to find an intuition whose manifold (color, shape, structure, etc.) matches what I take to be contained in my conceptual representation "tree."

---

[52] Most of Kant's examples attest to this.

[53] There is no direct textual evidence for my claim that the reflective scenario also gives rise both to a cognitive and an aesthetic reading, because Kant does not discuss the scenarios mentioned earlier as being distinct. My analysis of the reflective scenario is based on what I take to be implied in Kant's view that what he calls "subjective purposiveness" (§ 11) can be experienced, even when confronted with a nonconceptual representation and can therefore give rise to an aesthetic appraisal of the representation in question.

Here the intuition sought is the representation of an individual item of which I can be aware and which is in itself conceptually undetermined. Such an intuition is provided by the apprehending and comprehending activities of the power of imagination. Next I figure out whether there is an item that fits my concept of a tree or can be subsumed under the concept "tree" within the interminable domain of the intuitive material that the power of imagination provides. If yes, then I have successfully arrived at a cognition of an object, which means that I have confirmed that there is indeed something objectively around that corresponds to my concept of a tree and that the representation "tree" is not an empty, but an empirical concept through which an object can be determined.

In such a cognitive situation an interaction between the power of imagination and the understanding definitely takes place. This interaction is, however, not a free play of these two faculties. It is, according to Kant, initiated by my own intentional activity of putting both these faculties into operation in an effort to establish an agreement between them in order to arrive at the cognition of an object. After all, in such a situation I initiate this interaction because I have the intention of finding out whether the general representation "tree" supplied by the understanding is such that it accords with an intuitive item among the vast reservoir of intuitions, which are in turn produced by the power of imagination. In such a cognitive case the subject intentionally generates the interaction between the power of imagination and the understanding until they eventually agree, and thereby establishes what Kant calls an "intellectual consciousness [*intellektuelles Bewusstsein*]" of their relation (cf. *AA* 5, 218).[54] Thus, under these intellectual conditions essential to the cognitive situation in the determinative scenario, an agreement between the power of imagination and

---

[54] This intellectual consciousness occurs, if the starting point of the determination of a given representation is a concept, as Kant points out in one of his rather elliptical formulations: "Were the given representation . . . a concept that, in the appraisal of an object [*Gegenstand*] unified the understanding and the power of imagination into the cognition of an object [*Objekt*], then the consciousness of this relation would be intellectual" (ibid.).

the understanding turns out to be possible. Such an agreement is even necessary, if an object is to become available that can be conceptually determined. This agreement is, however, not founded in a free play of the two faculties, but is the result of an intentional action on the part of the subject that is guided by the input of the understanding. Such an action is inevitably accompanied by a cognitive (also called a logical: e.g., AA 5, 203, or a determining: e.g., AA 20, 223) judgment.

Given that aesthetic judgments have to be distinguished from cognitive judgments insofar as the former do not contribute to the objective determination of an object, Kant must maintain that an aesthetic interpretation of the determinative scenario is also possible. After all, he unambiguously holds that many of our aesthetic judgments involve attributing the predicate "beautiful" to something of which we have a conceptual representation present to our mind. How does he account for this possibility? According to Kant, one has to distinguish between an intellectual and an aesthetic consciousness of the agreement between the power of imagination and the understanding (ibid.). An aesthetic consciousness is meant to arise under circumstances where this agreement is not intellectually recognized, but is experienced emotionally through a certain feeling or sensation [Empfindung] of pleasure. This feeling is said to be a phenomenon of the "inner sense." It arises when the subject, while being aware of ("contemplating," cf. AA 5, 209) a given representation, senses its special kind of adequacy to what the power of imagination provides and the understanding demands in the attempt to think of it as a determinate object. Kant describes this feeling as occurring in the wake of an "enlivening of both faculties (the power of imagination and the understanding) to an undetermined though, in light of the given representation, harmonious activity, i.e. that [activity, R. P. H.] belongs to a cognition in general" (AA 5, 219). Whatever else it may mean, this statement makes clear that every given representation, be it a conceptual or an intuitive one, can occasion this feeling, if it is present under the right conditions. This implies that each of these kinds of representations allows for both a cognitive and an aesthetic response. Hence the determinative scenario, according to which the given representation is determined by a concept, must be open to both a cognitive and an aesthetic interpretation, if the original claim about the independence of aesthetic and cognitive judgments is to be upheld.

Kant seems to construe the situation in which an aesthetic judgment arises on analogy to what is happening in the cognitive interpretation of the determinative scenario. Here again the subject is aware of something that is determined by a conceptual representation, say, that of a tree. In contrast to the cognitive situation, in which the subject has to check whether the intuition that the power of imagination provides can be subsumed under the concept "tree," the aesthetic situation is such that there is an immediate match between the intuition the subject has and the concept it ponders. In an aesthetic situation one of two things, or both together, are most likely to occur: (1) the intuition meant to exhibit the given conceptual representation "tree" displays in an exemplary way all of the characteristics that the subject normally connects with what is contained in the concept of a tree; (2) the present intuition displays, over and above the "normal" characteristics, a host of features that the subject does not usually have in mind as contained in this concept, even though they do belong to this concept. In both cases the intuition displays a surplus, in case (1) a surplus of fittingness, in case (2) a surplus of characteristics of which I am usually unaware as being appropriate for determining an object as a tree.[55]

---

[55] I take it that P. Guyer (*Harmony of the Faculties Revisited.* In *Values of Beauty*, Cambridge: Cambridge University Press, 2005) wants to understand the interaction between the understanding and the power of imagination that gives rise to an aesthetic judgment in a similar way. Finding both the "precognitive" (Henrich, Ginsborg, Makkreel) and the "multicognitive" (G. Seel, Rush, Allison) interpretation of the harmony of faculty doctrine (81ff.) unconvincing, he holds that for Kant aesthetic judgments are about particular objects and thus depend on determinate concepts (their standard form is not "[t]his is beautiful," but "[t]his F is beautiful") (94ff.). This observation leads him to favor a "metacognitive" interpretation, according to which "we can . . . have ordinary cognition of the object, but we experience it as beautiful precisely because we

For an aesthetic situation to arise under these conditions, Kant seems to have the following in mind: I, the perceiving subject, recognize something that is in front of me as a sycamore tree. This recognition is an act of cognitively determining an object by subsuming an intuition apprehended and comprehended by the power of imagination under a conceptual representation provided by the understanding. In order to give rise to an aesthetic experience, in the case of (1), I have to notice that the sycamore in front of me displays the characteristics standardly connected with my conceptual representation of a sycamore tree *in the most exemplary way*. The hue of the grayish green color, the form of the leaves, the bulk of the trunk, and the thickness of the branches, etc. – all these marks displayed by the intuition not only match, but match most fittingly what is contained in my concept of a sycamore. It is as if the power of imagination, which is in charge of supplying this intuition, has made a special effort to come up with the actualization of an ideal token of my concept of a sycamore. This extraordinary fit between what is contained in my concept and what is provided by the power of imagination, a fit that exceeds what is necessary for correctly subsuming my intuition under my concept and thus for determining an object, is experienced by the subject as a contingent event of a particularly fortuitous interplay between the understanding and the power of imagination and is therefore accompanied by a feeling of pleasure. This harmonious interplay is not forced on these faculties by the subject as in a cognitive situation, but is a free play insofar as it happens by sheer chance that

experience it as inducing a degree or type of harmony between imagination and understanding – between the manifold it presents and our desire for unity – that goes beyond whatever is necessary for ordinary cognition" (99). I fully agree with this analysis of the Kantian view with respect to judgments of the form "[t]his F is beautiful," thus with respect to judgments that reflect the basic situation I call "the determinative scenario." I am, however, not as convinced that it can do justice to cases of "the reflective scenario," to cases where the aesthetic judgment has the form "[t]his is beautiful." This is so, I suppose, because Guyer would deny that these scenarios can be distinguished in the way I suggest. It seems that for him a judgment of the form "[t]his is beautiful" is just an elliptic way of judging "[t]his F is beautiful."

each of these faculties, acting independently of each other, none-theless complements each other in a most fruitful way.

A similar situation obtains in case (2). Here I realize that this sycamore present in intuition not only has the trunk, the branches, the leaves, and the mixture of colors characteristic of what is contained in my concept of such a tree, but that this intuition exhibits moreover many other characteristics I was not conscious were contained in my concept of a sycamore. Thus I might notice that the texture of the bark and the particular proportion between the trunk and the branches of this sycamore correspond in a paradigmatic fashion to what I expect on conceptual grounds a sycamore to display, though I was by no means aware that my concept of it did encompass these characteristics. In this situation, to put it metaphorically, the intuition proves to be much "richer," namely, to have more content than what the understanding deems necessary to integrate into its product, the concept of a sycamore. It is as if the understanding learns by chance something about its own product, something of which it has been hitherto unaware, on the fortuitous occasion of being given an intuition by the power of imagination that most perfectly fits the understanding's concept. Here again there is no intention by a subject involved. It just happens accidentally, without compulsion, that the power of ima-gination comes up with an intuitive item that perfectly fits the concept at hand. Thus here again we have a free play of the faculties, which is necessary for an aesthetic assessment of an object that results in a feeling of pleasure.

All of this is meant to show that Kant's views about the interac-tion between the faculties of the understanding and the power of imagination necessary for any appraisal [*Beurteilung*] of an object does indeed permit both a cognitive and an aesthetic interpreta-tion where the "given representation" is a concept, thus if the determinative scenario is taken to be the default scenario. It also turns out that, according to Kant, this interaction between these faculties is a "free play" only in the aesthetic interpretation of the determinative scenario, where no determining activities of the understanding are involved. But what about the reflective scenario? Can a reflective scenario also allow for a cognitive as well as an aesthetic interpretation, and is it also the case here that the interaction between the understanding and the power of imagination can be called "free" only in the aesthetic case?

It is easy to see that the reflective scenario mentioned earlier allows for an aesthetic interpretation, because it is based on what Kant describes as an "aesthetic consciousness" of the relation between the power of imagination and the understanding, and hence enables the subject to appraise [*beurteilen*] an object aesthetically. It is also easy to see that for Kant it is in this aesthetic context that the free play of the faculties is supposed to play a central role. So, how does an aesthetic experience arise under circumstances essential to the reflective scenario? The aesthetic situation, the state of affairs in which an aesthetic consciousness occurs, is characterized by the fact that the perceiving subject is aware exclusively of what the power of imagination provides – in other words, is conscious of an intuition of something without having the vaguest (conceptual) notion of what this intuition is an intuition of – and that this consciousness is accompanied by a feeling of pleasure. The situation Kant seems to have in mind might best be described by means of the normal perceptual circumstances. I, while looking at a painting, am aware only of a multitude of color patches that are next to each other and form a unified whole. I do not have the slightest idea what this assemblage of colors might signify, if it signifies anything at all. I just have the representation of a single colored whole, which is a representation with the status of an intuition. This intuition is the product of the power of imagination insofar as it is the result of the apprehending and comprehending activities of this faculty. Though this intuition "means" nothing to me, in the sense that it has no conceptual determinateness and hence determines no object, my experience of it can be such that I nonetheless feel [*empfinde*] that these color patches and their arrangement might be open to some conceptual interpretation for which this intuition is especially fitting. The intuitive representation contains, so to say, the *promise* of a specific concept that the understanding might be able to supply in order to transform it from a blind, conceptually empty intuition into the representation of an object. Whenever such a "bare" intuition present to me holds this promise of a significant match with a conceptual item that by itself is completely undetermined as to its content, it elicits a consciousness not of a harmony between itself and a determinate concept, which would be an intellectual consciousness and would indicate a cognitive setting. Instead, the consciousness stirred is an aesthetic consciousness based on an awareness of a correspondence between what the power of imagination, free from any demands imposed by other instances, has provided in the form of an intuition, and what the understanding could contribute in the form of a concept simply by operating in accordance with its own rules without aiming at conceptually determining a specific item. It is this latter consciousness, originating from the experience of the unforced harmony between the two cognitive faculties, that leads to the aesthetic judgment "this here, whatever it might be, is beautiful," and that is, according to Kant, accompanied by a feeling of pleasure.[56] Thus, the free play of the faculties is again the source of the possibility of an *aesthetic* experience of something that *as an intuition* is not yet a cognitive object, but could become one.

But this description of a situation in which an aesthetic assessment of a conceptually undetermined intuition takes place can be

---

[56] Here is an example of the situation I believe Kant has in mind in such a case. I am looking at one of these big Turner paintings of a sunrise from a certain distance. Even without having the slightest idea what the color patches that compose this painting are intended to represent, just by taking them in I can arrive at the aesthetic judgment "this conglomerate of colors in front of me is beautiful," accompanied by a feeling of pleasure. If I were asked, "why do you think so?", I would answer, "well, these color patches and their arrangement just look to me as if they were the most fitting realization of a concept that is on the tip of my tongue." If I were then told that this painting is meant to depict a sunrise, I might react by exclaiming: "Yes! That's it! This is the concept that exactly fits what I have been intuitively aware of, though that concept would never have occurred to me while looking at the painting." The point I want to make through this exchange is that I determine something (the collection of color patches), not through a concept, but simply through the pleasant feeling that this something is exceptionally well suited for exhibiting a concept that *in this situation* is unavailable to me.

convincing within the confines of a Kantian framework only if one acknowledges: (a) that there are intuitions around that cannot be transformed into representations of *objects*, and (b) that even those intuitions that could be transformed do not necessarily give rise to an aesthetic experience and stimulate the feeling of pleasure. If one does not agree to (a), one would have to accept that in principle every conceptually undetermined intuition, whether or not it is determinable, could become associated with an aesthetic feeling of pleasure and hence could occasion an aesthetic judgment. This does not seem to be Kant's view, because it would imply that the free play between the power of imagination and the understanding is connected with every intuition. If one were to deny (b), one would have to blur the distinction between an aesthetic experience and a cognitive assessment of something that could become the representation of an object. One would have to hold that every attempt to cognitively assess a conceptually undetermined intuition would unavoidably bring with it an aesthetic experience. This view also cannot be attributed to Kant, because he thinks of aesthetic responses to given representations as being responses sui generis that are independent of cognitive assessments of these representations.

This leads to the second, cognitive interpretation of the reflective scenario. Here the initial situation is the same as in the aesthetic case. The perceiving subject is aware exclusively of what the power of imagination provides and is conscious of an intuition of something without having the vaguest (conceptual) notion of what this intuition is an intuition of. In this case, however, there is no feeling of pleasure involved. This is so because in the cognitive case there is no, metaphorically speaking, enjoyable play between the power of imagination and the understanding, but they engage jointly in hard work. Here I am aware of an indefinite item, a "this," somewhere in the distance. I have no clue under which concept I can subsume this item, though I have the frustrating feeling that if I were to search long enough, I definitely would find a concept that fits it. So I feel compelled to explore which concept could be fitting. This is a matter of trial and error. I run through different conceptual representations, assess whether any of the marks found in the intuition correspond to what is contained in the concept I tentatively entertain, I exclude one candidate after another, until I eventually reach a result that culminates in the cognitive judgment "[t]his 'this' in front of me is a tree." The power of imagination and the understanding are undeniably implicated in this process because the power of imagination makes the intuition available, the understanding provides the candidate concepts, and their activities refer mutually to each other. In this case they pursue a common task, namely, the cognitive task of determining an object. They do not, however, play freely with each other. They are instead bound to collaborate in an effort to find a match between an intuition and a concept in order to come to a conclusive result, a conceptually fixed representation. And although I might feel relaxed after I have arrived at this result, I do not have to be pleased. Maybe the appropriate emotional attitude would be a feeling of satisfaction at my success. But there is no room for a genuine aesthetic response.

This brief excursion into different interpretations of the interaction between the two faculties was carried out in order to emphasize two points relevant to Kant's views concerning the modus operandi of the power of imagination in the context of the constitution of cognitive objects. The first is that he considers the power of imagination and the understanding to be of equal weight when it comes to the formation of representations of objects about which (cognitive and/or aesthetic) judgments can be made. They are of equal weight because both of them are necessary for producing object representations. But they are furthermore on an equal footing because each of them can act independently of the other, not just in the sense that they pursue different tasks, but also in the sense that they can perform their task-related actions in splendid isolation. The second is that, even in a situation where this interaction can be called a "free play," neither the power of imagination nor the understanding is meant to operate without being bound by any rules whatsoever. They play freely not *with* themselves, but *from* each other. Playing freely just means that their rule-bound activities happen to lead unintentionally to a contingent correspondence between their otherwise necessary contributions to the representation of a determinate object.[57]

## 2.3 Schemata and the Freedom of the Power of Imagination

Kant's theory of the free play of the cognitive faculties in aesthetic appreciation corroborates our previous discovery of an implicit claim in both editions of the first *Critique* – the claim that the power of imagination is a self-standing cognitive faculty. It can operate independently from the rules of the understanding in the pursuit of its genuine and exclusive task of generating intuitions. Its activity is not restricted to providing intuitions of objects, but is allowed to produce simply "blind" intuitions, whether they are conceptualizable or not. The theory of the free play thus can be

---

[57] An interesting consequence of this understanding of the free play is that such free play on its own need not be or lead to the specific harmony between the power of imagination and the understanding associated with an aesthetic experience. The free play, though harmonious in the sense that it indicates the general suitability of what each of these faculties can provide for the constitution of a representation of an object, is not enough to constitute an aesthetic harmony between the operations of these faculties. This general suitability does not necessarily lead to a perfect fit between the products of their interaction. The free play as a condition for an aesthetic response to an object representation might as well end in a "discord" [*Misshelligkeit*] between the power of imagination and the understanding, and hence issue in a feeling of frustration instead. Kant addresses this possibility of a bad fit between these faculties in his characterization of a critique of taste in § 34: "it is the art or science of bringing the reciprocal relation of the understanding and the power of imagination in the given representation . . ., consequently their unanimity or discord under rules and to determine them [rules, R. P. H.] in consideration of their conditions" (*AA* 5, 286). The possibility that even a discord within the free play of the faculties can give rise to an aesthetic judgment is for Kant an indicator that aesthetic judgments are not restricted to those that indicate a perfect fit between what the power of imagination and the understanding provides. This possibility of discord opens a way, not only for an aesthetics of the sublime, but possibly even for an "aesthetics of ugliness" in Kant's theory.

seen as indirectly confirming the view defended in the preceding sections; viz. that Kant thinks of cognitive object constitution as a process that runs through different stages, the first of which necessarily involves the power of imagination without limiting it to the production of a special kind of intuitions, i.e. intuitions of objects. If one were to use the terminology Kant favored in the first *Critique*, one could say that the third *Critique* confirms the view that for him the power of imagination is confined neither to its object-constituting or transcendental function, nor to its reproductive capacities, but that it is above all a productive capacity aimed at generating intuitions that might be, but need not be representations of objects.

Kant's comments about the free play of the faculties in the third *Critique* can also shed some light on his rather obscure and confusing remarks concerning figurative synthesis as the distinctive feature of the productive power of imagination in the *Transcendental Deduction* of the B-edition of the first *Critique*. The relevant sentences in § 24 state: "This synthesis of the manifold of the sensible intuition that is possible and necessary a priori can be called figurative (synthesis speciosa) . . . However, figurative synthesis if aiming only at the original synthetic unity of apperception that is thought in the categories must . . . be named the transcendental synthesis of the power of imagination" (*CpR*, B 151). Understood against the background of this free play, one can take him to point to a needed distinction between the specific ways in which the productive power of imagination fulfills its function when engaged in its primary task of synthesizing a given manifold into an intuition. Kant seems to hold that, generally speaking, this synthetic activity of the productive power of imagination can only take place under two conditions. The first is that the power of imagination is bound to operate under the constraints given by the forms of sensibility (space and time). The second is that the power of imagination has to comply with the general demand on an item in order for it to become something the subject is conscious of. This means that the power of imagination has to "determine a priori the sense with respect to its form in accordance with the unity of apperception" (*CpR*, B 152).

If these two conditions are met, then one can specify the synthetic function that the productive power of imagination is meant to fulfill as consisting in the giving of a spatiotemporal *form* (a spatial figure or a temporal sequence) to what it brings together into the *unity* of an intuition. Or, to put it differently, this synthetic function consists in subjecting the given manifold to a *figurative* synthesis whose outcome is a *unitary* intuition. But to bring a manifold in accordance with the unity of apperception into a spatiotemporal form (a figure, a sequence) and thus make it an intuition does not imply forming the intuition of an *object*, which is an item whose form agrees with that unity "which is thought in the categories" (*CpR*, B 151). A unified spatiotemporal manifold could as well be an indeterminate patch of color or an unmelodic string of sounds whose unity is categorially completely undetermined. Such an intuition could not be taken to be an intuition of a cognitive object. For that, an intuition would have to be the outcome of a synthesis by the power of imagination taking place "in accordance with the categories" (*CpR*, B 152). Kant calls this synthesis of a spatiotemporal manifold into an intuition according to the categories "transcendental synthesis of the imagination" (ibid.), since it is by means of the categories that representations of *objects* are generated, and whatever contributes (a priori) to the formation of the representation of an object is for him a transcendental item. Thus the transcendental synthesis of imagination can be understood as specifying what the power of imagination does with data anyway, which is to synthesize them figuratively into spatiotemporal forms. This interpretation can even account for Kant's talk of the transcendental status of an "intellectual synthesis" (ibid.). If synthesis is performed in abstraction from a spatiotemporal framework by the understanding alone and takes place solely "with regard to the manifold of an intuition in general thought in the pure [*bloßen*] category" (*CpR*, 151), then it is still a transcendental synthesis because it is still executed in accordance with (some of) the requirements of cognitive object constitution. But insofar as it is one-sided by abstracting away from the sensibility condition, it is a purely intellectual synthesis of the understanding.[58]

Kant's observations concerning the free play of the cognitive faculties are obviously guided by the firm belief that the power of imagination acts independently from the understanding while dealing with a given manifold of sensible data in order to establish representations of individual items. This independence makes the interaction between the power of imagination and the understanding a free play. But to be able to act free *from* the constraints of the understanding does not mean to be entitled *to* act freely, in the sense of acting unbounded by any rules. It could well be the case that, though they act freely from one another, both the power of imagination and the understanding pursue their respective activities in a way that is regulated by a fixed set of procedures that grants them no freedom at all. In the case of the understanding, Kant explicitly confirms that all its synthesizing activities are rule-bound in that they synthesize the intuitive material according to laws codified in the categories. After all, as he repeatedly points out, the understanding is the faculty that is governed by the a priori principle of lawfulness [*Gesetzmäßigkeit*] (cf. *AA* 5, 319, 198), which implies that it does not act freely.

---

[58] My reading of Kant's first *Critique* views concerning figurative and intellectual synthesis seems to me to be in accordance with the way in which B. Longuenesse interprets this distinction in her *Kant and the Capacity to Judge* (202ff.). It disagrees, however, with W. Waxman's (*Kant's Anatomy of the Intelligent Mind*, 382) assessment, according to which "the transcendental synthesis directed at the manifold of space and time (the *synthesis speciosa* of the B Deduction) must be conceived as a specification (to spatial and temporal content) of a more fundamental, purely discursive synthesis grounded on pure concepts of the understanding (the *synthesis intellectualis* of the B Deduction)." Though one could call the relation between these two syntheses a specification, I see no reason to think of synthesis intellectualis as more fundamental. It is just a synthesis "in accordance with the categories" (*CpR*, B 152) that has the defect of neglecting the sensibility condition. My reading is also in tension with S. Gibbons's suggestion (*Kant's Theory of Imagination*) "that the viability of a strict distinction between these and the desirability of such a distinction is questionable" (39). Contrary to her, I take this distinction to be both desirable and viable.

But what about the power of imagination? Is there also a set of law-like rules that determine its activities and thus preclude its acting freely while engaged in a "free play"? Or to put this question differently, does the power of imagination possess something like a self-standing freedom, not just in its capacity to form intuitions, but also when its activity is subject to the condition that it lead to conceptualizable results? If framed the latter way, the answer is yes. In many passages in the aesthetic part of the third *Critique*, he unambiguously asserts that the power of imagination acts freely, not just from the rules of the understanding, but from (almost) any rules (cf. *AA* 5, 230, 241, 242, 256), except of course those that relate to determination in time.[59] He even characterizes the freedom the activity of the power of imagination enjoys as amounting to a free play (e.g., *AA* 5, 256, 230). However, and this is the decisive point, this freedom has to be exercised under a very peculiar condition or within very special limits, for its exercise has to take place in a process where the power of imagination is geared toward providing intuitions that are at least in principle conceptualizable. It is only if the power of imagination can be seen as engaged in the activity of providing intuitive material to the understanding that the unrestricted freedom at stake here can be attributed to it. This suggests that the manifold the power of imagination "in its freedom" is compelled to combine into a conceptually undetermined intuition that can be manipulated in various ways, as long as the resulting product is an intuition that is in principle conceptualizable and so can be related to the

---

[59] In the end it is hard to decide if Kant wants to endorse the positive claim that there are no rules that guide the activities of the power of imagination in exercising its freedom, or if he is agnostic as to whether there are such rules. I tend to think that he wants to avoid an unambiguous stance on this question. After all, in the first *Critique* he already states (in connection with an assessment of the schematizing activities of the power of imagination) that these schematizing operations are "a concealed art [*verborgene Kunst*] in the depths of the human soul whose modes of operation [*Handgriffe*] we will hardly find out [*ablernen*] from nature and lay open to the eyes [*unverdeckt vor Augen legen*]" (A 141/B 180 f.).

"understanding with its lawfulness" (*AA* 5, 287).[60] A closer look at how Kant conceives of this freedom of the power of imagination to manipulate items *under the condition of the conceptualizability of the resulting intuition* confirms this suggestion.

In order to find out what this self-standing freedom of the power of imagination might consist in, one has to turn to Kant's aesthetic theory and revisit his original sketch from both the first and the third *Critiques* of how the cognitive faculties operate in the formation of the representation of an object. In both texts, the basic assumption is that in order to bring about representations of objects, the power of imagination has to provide the understanding with organized material that has the status of intuitions. Kant makes very clear that this organization into what can count as an intuition is the result of a synthesis. This means that, if a freedom is to be attributed to the power of imagination, it must be grounded in the way the power of imagination can perform its syntheses. In the third *Critique* Kant characterizes this special activity of synthesis distinctive of the power of imagination somewhat vaguely as "aesthetic comprehension" (*AA* 5, 251). As was already mentioned, this aesthetic comprehension brings together a given manifold of sensible data into an intuition where what is meant by intuition is just a "whole representation" [*ganze Vorstellung*] (*AA* 18, 320) that possesses a certain shape [*Gestalt*] (cf. *AA* 5, 225) and is hence an indeterminate (though intentional) object [*unbestimmter Gegenstand*]. Aesthetic comprehension can be called "free" because there is no concept required for this formative process. Hence the resulting intuition does not necessarily have to be the intuition of a cognitive object, an object about which objectively valid judgments can be made.

But this freedom of the power of imagination in aesthetic comprehension does not seem to be the specific freedom Kant has in

---

[60] This suggests that, within the Kantian picture of faculty involvement in aesthetic and cognitive judgments, one has to relate the free play of the faculties in their interaction to the free play peculiar to the power of imagination. This means that the free play of the power of imagination must be such that it enables a free play between the faculties.

mind when it comes to the operations of the power of imagination that are accessible to the understanding and can lead to a free play between these faculties. After all, this comprehending activity takes place completely independent of any involvement of the understanding, and so cannot be seen as aiming to provide intuitions to the understanding for the sake of its conceptualizing activity. In other words, the shaped compilations of a manifold produced by aesthetic comprehension, such as an indefinite patch of color or a senseless sequence of letters, though produced free from any involvement by the understanding, are not generated with a view to the conditions of their conceptualizability. They are indifferent to whether or not the understanding can relate to them in the attempt to conceptualize them. Intuitions viewed as mere products of aesthetic comprehension are not only blind, they also remain blind unless the "power of imagination in its freedom awakens the understanding, and it [the understanding, R. P. H.] without concepts puts the power of imagination into a measured [*regelmäßiges*] play" (*AA* 5, 296).

The freedom Kant has in mind must be of another kind. It must be a kind of freedom that can be attributed to the power of imagination in its endeavor to provide formed material (intuitions) within reach of the understanding's conceptualization. Because every activity of the understanding is bound to be rule-governed, the imputed freedom of the power of imagination in the process of giving its material the form of an intuition must belong to it in its capacity to generate conceptualizable items. It must be a freedom that belongs to the power of imagination if it is viewed as operating under conditions that can in principle lead to results accessible to the activities of the understanding – or, in Kant's words, can "awaken the understanding" (ibid.), without guidance from the understanding.

These sophisticated constraints leave only narrow options for finding a fitting kind of synthesizing activity of the power of imagination. One learns from both the first and the third *Critique* that the functions Kant expects the power of imagination to perform range from achieving aesthetic comprehension via figurative and transcendental synthesis, to the task of schematizing for the sake and under the auspices of the understanding. Within this wide spectrum, there seems to be only one that can at least approximately be interpreted as pertaining to the special way he wants the understanding to be simultaneously present and absent while the power of imagination is at work. Aesthetic comprehension as well as figurative synthesis are functions of the power of imagination that do not require any contribution of the understanding, while the transcendental synthesis of the power of imagination positively requires its contribution in the guise of the categories. Because there is either too much or too little contribution of the understanding in both cases, these activities fall short of the kind of freedom of which Kant takes the power of imagination to be capable.

This leaves the schematizing activities of this power. As we are told in the "Schematism" chapter of the first *Critique, in cognitive contexts* these activities consist in providing the means or method [*Verfahren*] "of supplying a concept with its image" (*CpR*, A 140/B 179 f.). This is done by making a schema available, which is a rule for the understanding according to which a given expanse of sensible data can be thought of as exemplifying or "realizing" a concept (cf. *CpR*, A 147/B 187). If there is an empirical or even a pure sensible (mathematical) concept at hand, then the schema determines to what this concept can relate in the domain of sensible data. In this way the schema determines what the understanding can rely on in order to give an intuitively accessible interpretation of that concept in the guise of an image, thereby providing evidence for its non-emptiness. Kant takes these schemata, as well as the images [*Bilder*] enabled by them, to be products of the power of imagination while operating under the guidance of the understanding (*CpR*, A 140 f./B 179 f.). If this schematizing process takes place in order to secure an image for a given concept, then the power of imagination cannot be said to act freely. But what about contexts in which no concept is given and the power of imagination pursues its business of combining sensible data into a whole (aesthetic comprehension) without being constrained by the demand to produce a procedure according to which an image can be found for a specific concept? Then it would seem that this schematizing activity could be called free, if it operates under the conditions (1) that no concept guides this activity and, (2) that it nevertheless stimulates or awakens the faculty of concepts (cf., e.g., *AA* 5, 228) to come up with a concept.

Based on such a line of thought, one has some reasons to expect that the freedom Kant attributes to the power of imagination consists in its ability to schematize freely. And this is exactly what Kant states, though hidden in a subordinate clause of a sentence in a passage in § 35 of the third *Critique*. The passage in question deals with the peculiarities of a judgment of taste: "Because here no concept of the object is the basis of the judgment, it [the judgment, R. P. H.] can consist only in the subsumption of the power of imagination itself (in the case of a representation whereby an object is given) under the condition that the understanding in general arrives from an intuition at concepts, i.e. *because the freedom of the power of imagination consists precisely in that it schematizes without concept* [italics, R. P. H.]: the judgment of taste has to be based on a mere sensation of the reciprocal vitalization of the power of imagination in its freedom and the understanding with its lawfulness, i.e. in a feeling" (*AA* 5, 287). But to be informed that the power of imagination is free because it has the ability to schematize without concepts might be considered unhelpful, as long as one is not additionally told what this characterization amounts to. Here again Kant seems reluctant to supply any details. Although he mentions schemata in § 59 of the third *Critique* in the context of "hypotypose (*Darstellung*)," and dwells upon the distinction between a schematic manner of representing [*schematische Vorstellungsart*] and a symbolic one, he does not resume the topic of the schematizing activity of the power of imagination in the third *Critique*. Thus one is compelled to return to his sketchy comments on the schematism of the understanding in the first *Critique* in an attempt to discover what he means by his talk of schematizing without concept.

In the first *Critique* the theory of the schematism of the understanding is designed to solve the problem of the applicability of concepts to objects of experience (appearances). As Kant sees it, the problem is a consequence of his claims, (a) that there is an irreducible difference between the faculties of sensibility and understanding because of their heterogeneity and, (b) that every cognition is the joint product of both faculties because it connects conceptual and intuitive elements. Now, concepts are the result of the synthesizing activity of the understanding, and intuitions are produced by the power of imagination from material provided by sensibility, while cognition consists in a judgment that has objective meaning because the concepts involved can be related to an intuition. How, then, can such a relation between concepts and intuitions ever be established? It is well known that Kant believes he can solve this problem by introducing mediating representations between concepts and intuitions that are partly homogeneous with conceptual representations on one hand, and partly homogenous with intuitive representations on the other. Since concepts as general representations share the essential mark of generality [*Allgemeinheit*], and intuitions (as individual representations of a manifold of data ordered in time) share the mark of temporality, a mediating representation between concepts and intuitions has to capture these two characteristics (cf. *CpR*, A 137/B 176ff.). He calls such a mediating representation a "schema," and takes it to be a product of the power of imagination (*CpR*, A 140/B 179). Given that concepts on their own are just rules that unite a number of marks into the representation of an object in general, and intuitions on their own are just representations of concept-less unifications of sensuous element in the shape of a whole [*Ganzes*] in general,[61] the function of these schemata is to specify conceptual rules in such a way that these

---

[61] Concepts of objects in general, as well as intuitions in general, have to be distinguished from spatiotemporal concepts of objects and spatiotemporal intuitions. The former pair, though categorially determined, lacks spatiotemporal determination. In other words, objects and intuitions *in general* are undetermined with respect to conditions of sensibility, whereas the latter pair already conforms to conditions imposed by *our* sensibility (cf. § 22 of the B Deduction, *CpR*, B 146 f., also A 93/B 125 f.).

rules can refer to intuitive wholes subject to the time condition. Such a specification of conceptual rules is necessary so that a human being who intuits within a (spatio)temporal framework can arrive at the representation of a spatiotemporal object, not just of an object in general. All of this makes perfectly good sense, as long as one is willing to accept the Kantian conviction that there will never be a representation of an object present to the mind that is not conceptually determined, even though every mind contains countless representations that are conceptually undetermined and maybe even undeterminable. For Kant the very term "concept-less object" would be a *contradictio in adiecto*. Hence concepts as rules of unification can play their epistemic role only if there is an interpretation of them that makes them "sensible concepts" [*sinnliche Begriffe*], i.e. schemata (cf. *CpR*, A 146/B 186).

Kant's epistemic universe has many kinds of concepts, such as, for instance, the aesthetic, ethical, mathematical, transcendental, and empirical concepts. Does his theory of the schematism of the understanding imply that all of these concept types are subject to schematization before they can be used in order to determine whatever it is to which they are meant to refer? If they refer to possible objects of cognition, which are objects that can be exhibited [*dargestellt*] in space and time, the answer is yes. Of those on the list, at least transcendental, mathematical, and empirical concepts would be subject to schematization as a condition of their applicability, since they are involved in the process of cognitive object constitution. There is, however, a difference in the manner in which they perform this task, depending on the role they are designed to play in this process. Transcendental concepts are meant to be constitutive of the representation of an object in general; mathematical concepts are meant to determine mathematical objects; and empirical concepts have the function of giving rise to the representation of empirical objects. Each of these concept types will be in need of a schema if they are to achieve their goal, i.e. prove applicable to objects conforming to the conditions of our sensibility in that they can be thought of as objects in space and time.[62]

As was already pointed out, concepts by themselves are simply rules that can establish synthetic unities. If schematizing is indeed a necessary condition for the applicability of these rules, and if the power of imagination carries out this task, then it seems that the schematizing activity of the power of imagination must produce a distinct kind of schema for each of the different types of object-constituting concepts. This raises the questions: what are these kinds of schema and how does the imagination establish them? In the case of transcendental concepts, the categories, Kant's suggestion seems to be that the power of imagination transforms these concepts into rules of temporal connectivity [*Verbindbarkeit*] of sensibly given material or sense data.[63] Such a transformation generates a schematic rule that determines the way in which the conceptual relations contained in the purely logical meaning of a categorial concept – the meaning a category has independently of its applicability to spatiotemporal material – must be reinterpreted, if such a categorial concept is to be useful in the process of ordering spatiotemporal material into the representation of an item of which cognition is possible, whether object or intuition.

[62] A similar point is made by J. Haag (*Erfahrung und Gegenstand.* Klostermann Verlag: Frankfurt 2007, 279 ff.), who also allows for transcendental, pure (mathematical), and empirical schemata. But he gives the entire schematism a different interpretation from mine in that he tries to explicate the meaning and the function of the schemata within a framework that is strongly influenced by W. Sellars's work, especially by Sellars's *The Role of Imagination in Kant's Theory of Experience*. In H. Johnstone, ed., *Categories: A Colloquium.* Philadelphia, PA: Pennsylvania State University Press, 1978, 231 ff. Consequently the concept of an image model becomes central to Haag's reading.

[63] This is meant to be a rephrasing of a formulation Kant uses in the "Schematism" chapter: "The schemata are ... nothing but time-determinations a priori according to rules" (*CpR*, A 145/B 184). Similarly in the second *Critique* he characterizes the schema of a category as "a general procedure of the power of imagination (to exhibit the pure concept of the understanding ... a priori to the senses)" (*AA* 5, 69).

In order to get a better sense of what Kant has in mind, it might help to look at his preferred examples, the categories of cause and substance. According to Kant, the concept of cause, when abstracted from its empirical application, connotes the rule that there must be a (logical) ground–consequence relation between two items. But in order to become applicable to items present in space and time, it has to be modified into a rule that can capture these sensible peculiarities of the items at hand, their spatiotemporal character. This modification is carried out by the power of imagination by temporalizing [*verzeitlichen*] the logical ground–consequence relation into the cause–effect relation between two items, according to which the one has to follow the other in time, thereby transforming a logical relation between terms (concepts, judgments) into a "real" relation between spatiotemporal entities (events, state of affairs) (cf. *CpR*, A 90/B 122 and *Prolegomena*, § 29 f. [*AA* 4, 312]).[64] Hence the schema of the concept of cause is the procedure by which the power of imagination establishes the rule of necessary succession in time of whatever is causally related.

As far as the schematization of the category of substance is concerned, Kant again wants us to consider the requirements of its applicability. He holds that the concept of substance on its own, without any specification of the conditions for its application, amounts to the rule that something should be thought of only as

---

[64] Going back to a suggestion by R. Butts (*Kant's Schemata as Semantical Rules*. In L. W. Beck, ed., *Kant Studies Today*. LaSalle, IL: Open Court Press, 1969, 290–300), this procedure is sometimes interpreted in terms of the distinction between a syntax and a semantics of a language. This analogy is indeed helpful, if restricted to Kant's pure concepts of the understanding, namely, the categories understood as concepts that make the very representation of an object possible. It can even be seen as suggested by Kant's metaphorical statement in the *Prolegomena* (§ 30), according to which the pure concepts of the understanding "serve as it were only to spell out appearances, so that they can be read as experience" (*AA* 4, 312). In the case of mathematical and empirical concepts, however, the syntax-semantics comparison might be less appropriate, because these concepts are even in their unschematized form semantically "loaded." Their "logical" in the sense of unschematized meaning already relies on their embeddedness in a spatiotemporal framework of sensible appearances, and hence already relies on a space-time semantics.

a first subject, a subject that can never be a predicate. But the relation between subject and predicate is only a logical (conceptual) relation. To make this rule applicable to spatiotemporal items, we need a procedure to uncover "which determinations a [spatiotemporal, R. P. H.] thing has that has to count as such a first subject" (*CpR*, A 147/B 187). This procedure is provided by the power of imagination and results in the sensible rule [*sinnliche Regel*], according to which only those items can count as a substance within the realm of the sensibly given that are persistent in time relative to what can change (cf. *CpR*, A 143/B 183). The power of imagination is once again supposed to transform a purely logical rule, which on its own does not indicate how it must be modified in order to become applicable to material given in a spatiotemporal framework, into a rule capable of contributing to the determination of a given manifold of intuitions. It does so by discriminating whether this manifold can qualify as representation of a substance and hence as (part of) the representation of a cognitive object. Such a rule determines whether this manifold can be "subsumed" (as Kant calls it, though this term is not adequate to the situation at hand[65]) under the concept of a substance.[66]

[65] E. R. Curtius, ("*Das Schematismuskapitel in der Kritik der reinen Vernunft.*" *Kant Studien* 19, 1914, 338–366) convincingly showed more than 100 years ago that Kant's attempt to present the need for schematization as rooted in the problem of subsumption is misleading.

[66] I can be excused for providing such a shallow outline of his theory of the schematization of the categories when compared to his own presentation of it. In his desire to squeeze all even remotely relevant considerations into one sentence, he often comes up with formulations that are nearly incomprehensible. An outstanding example of such an inimitably obscure and condensed formulation is the sentence that has the overambitious task of spelling out, not just what a schema of a category is, but also what is involved in the process of establishing such a schema. It merits being quoted: "the schema of a pure concept of the understanding is something that can be brought into no image whatsoever, but is solely the pure synthesis according to a rule of unity in accordance with concepts in general which the category expresses, and is a transcendental product of the power of imagination which concerns the determination of inner sense in general according to conditions of its form (of time) with respect to all representations insofar as these [representations, R. P. H.] in accordance with the unity of apperception should hang together

In the case of mathematical (geometrical and arithmetical) concepts, the situation is a bit different. Kant seems to conceive of the schemata of these concepts not primarily as rules that make the very concept of a spatiotemporal object available, but as rules provided by the power of imagination for constructing *images* of concepts with a spatiotemporal connotation, because of their reference to objects understood as specifications of the pure (*not* empirical) intuitions of space and time. Here, again, a look at his favorite examples might be of use. These are the geometrical concept of a triangle and the arithmetical concept of the number 5. The geometrical concept "triangle" designates every figure enclosing a space within the boundaries of three lines. There are, however, infinitely many different objects that satisfy this characterization (in other words, all triangles), each of which can give rise to a specific sensible intuition or can be represented in a specific image. What justifies the application of one and the same concept "triangle" to all of these different images is the fact that there is a regular and uniform procedure or rule that specifies the conditions necessary for the generation of an image of a triangle in terms of operations performed in the medium of space and time (such as drawing lines, measuring angles, etc.). This constructive rule is a product of the power of imagination. It is a rule, a "schema," that sensualizes [*versinnlichen*] the concept "triangle" and serves as the means for the construction of images, thereby giving this concept a basis in sensibility.

Kant provides a similar line of reasoning with respect to the arithmetical concept "5". I can visualize the concept "5" in many different images, such as five points on a piece of paper, five apples

a priori in a concept" (*CpR*, A 142/B 181). What exactly this statement amounts to is not obvious, to say the least. Hence it is unsurprising that there are significant differences among the major English translations of this sentence (Meiklejohn, Kemp-Smith, Pluhar, Guyer/Wood). Kant's basic idea, however, becomes more accessible in the examples he provides. As far as I know, the two most extensive and detailed reconstructions of how Kant arrives at the specific schemata he correlates to each category are to be found in B. Longuenesse, *Kant and the Capacity to Judge*, 243ff. and W. Waxman, *Kant and the Intelligent Mind*, 327ff.

in a basket, five fingers, etc. But these images have to be distinguished both from the concept "5" and from its schema. The concept "5" on its own is just the representation of a specific manifold of unities [*Menge von Einheiten*]. In order for this specific unity to become relatable to something sensible in space and time, namely, to an image-like [*bildhafte*] representation, one has to come up with "the representation of a method to represent according to a certain concept [in this case the concept "5", R. P. H.] a multitude . . . in an image" (*CpR*, A 140/B 179). This method is the schema of the concept "5", which carries the burden of ensuring that there can be something in space and time (something that can be represented in an image) to which the concept "5" can be applied, thus giving it an objective meaning. If we do not have a schematic rule to attach to a concept, then this concept is simply empty. In the terms of Frege's distinction, this concept might have sense, but not meaning.[67]

This leaves empirical concepts. The process of empirical concept formation involves the operations of comparison, abstraction, and reflection (cf. *Logik, AA* 9, 93ff.), operations that have to be performed on intuitions of what is given in space and time. This means that empirical concepts are already based on the presence of sensible intuitions, which suggests that there is no need to establish schemata for them in order to have the means to apply them to empirical objects. Rather, it seems that the very fact that they are *empirical* concepts guarantees their applicability to material that has to be given in space and time. One could get the impression that, if one follows Kant's outline of what a schema has to achieve,

---

[67] Kant's one sentence description of the schema of a mathematical as well as an empirical concept reads as follows: "the schema of sensible concepts (as of figures in space) [is, R. P. H.] a product and as it were a monogram of the pure power of imagination a priori through which and in accordance with which the images are first of all possible which [images, R. P. H.] however have to be connected with the concept by means of the schema that they [the images, R. P. H.] denote and [which, i.e. the images, R. P. H.] by itself are not completely congruent to it [i.e., the schema, R. P. H.]" (*CpR*, A 141 f./B 181). Kant tries to elucidate his point with respect to mathematical concepts in §§ 10 to 13 of the *Prolegomena* and the notes accompanying them (cf. *AA* 4, 283ff.).

empirical concepts provide no basis for distinguishing between concepts and schemata. Kant insists, however, that empirical concepts do also have schemata: "Even less so [viz. than a mathematical object, R. P. H.] does an object of experience or image of it ever attain the empirical concept, but the latter [i.e., the concept, R. P. H.] refers always immediately to the schema of the power of imagination as a rule of the determination of our intuition in accordance with a particular general concept" (*CpR*, A 141/B 180). This remark poses a puzzle, since it gives no hint as to why and how a schema of an empirical concept has to be established.

The idea behind this statement could be the following: The empirical concept contains a number of the characteristics of an empirical object. These characteristics are obtained from comparing numerous objects, reflecting on what they have in common, and abstracting from their differences. In this manner we generate a list of properties that characterize the objects that fall under the concept to which they give rise. This list contains what is often called the "intension" of a concept. It does not, however, address the way these characteristics have to be ordered in space and time in order to make the concept applicable to a spatiotemporally given object or to its image. In other words, the items on this list leave undetermined how they would have to be arranged in order to result in an image of the object that the concept is meant to determine.[68] Thus, to expand on an example Kant has in mind, my empirical concept of a dog will contain the connotations "animal," "four-footed," "furry," "ears," "tail," among others. This list is neutral with respect to the way these marks have to hang together in a spatiotemporal framework, if they are to represent an empirical object that falls under the concept "dog." In order to make this concept applicable to a "given manifold" of sensible data, one first has to establish a rule according to which this manifold can be organized in space and time in such a way that the ears are connected to a head and not to

---

[68] An informative discussion of why schematization has to take place and how Kant conceives of transcendental schemata, as well as of schemata of empirical concepts, is to be found in R. Pippin, "The Schematism and Empirical Concepts." *Kant Studien* 67, 1976, 156–171.

a tail, the feet are affixed underneath and not above a body, the fur enwraps a body and not the other way round, etc. In short, before the empirical concept "dog" can be applied, the space-time relations of the marks contained in this concept have to be fixed by a connectivity rule. Such a rule is a schema of this concept and represents "a general procedure of the power of imagination to supply a concept with its image" (*CpR*, A 140/B 179 f.).

We can learn the following lesson from this short excursion into Kant's views about schemata and their function in the first *Critique*: even though the power of imagination is responsible for providing schemata to the mind, it is not fully free in the process of establishing a schema, because these schemata depend on which concept the understanding wants schematized. When it comes to the schematization of concepts, the understanding takes precedence because it provides the concepts to which a schema is to be established. To put it metaphorically, the understanding "commissions" the power of imagination to find a sensible pattern that fits the marks specified by the concept in question, a pattern that this concept needs in order to gain objective significance. In other words, schematization occurs as soon as the *understanding* wants to relate anything conceptual (be it in the guise of a categorial or of a mathematical or even of an empirical concept) to something that is presentable to us in accordance with our conditions of sensibility. This makes schematization a "schematism of the understanding" (*CpR*, A 145/B 185), namely, a process that the power of imagination carries out in the service of the understanding.

Against the background of this picture of the power of imagination *in cognitive contexts*, Kant's remark in the third *Critique* that the freedom of the power of imagination consists in its capacity to schematize *without* concept becomes even more puzzling. So what could the freedom to schematize without concepts, to provide schemata for something that is conceptually undetermined, mean, if a schema is the "representation of a general procedure of the power of imagination to supply a concept with its image" (*CpR*, 140/B 179 f.)? Two points are immediately clear. First, schematizing without concept can only be attributed to the power of imagination when active in the empirical domain of what is sensibly given, since it is only in this realm that the power of imagination can find material that is inherently independent of anything conceptual – sense data. Second, the schema established by the activities of the power of imagination, when schematizing without a concept at hand, has to be achieved through operations the power of imagination performs on sensibly given material alone, prior to any conceptual guidance. Otherwise there would be a violation of the condition that nothing conceptual should be involved in the process of forming rules that can function as schemata.

If one is prepared to accept these two points, as well as the foregoing description of a schema as establishing a relation between an image and a concept, then the power of imagination in its original pursuit of ordering a manifold of sensible data into some intuitive pattern must deliver an intuitive item that can be taken to be an image[69] on which the understanding can perform its operations for the sake of concept formation.

For the power of imagination to schematize without concepts would then just mean for it to be able – while pursuing its primary task of comprehending [*zusammenbringen*] a given manifold of sensible data in order to produce intuitions – to launch the reverse process to that of schematizing under the guidance of a concept provided by the understanding. In the latter process the power of imagination is forced to arrange a schema necessary for a concept that is already present in the mind by allotting an intuitive image to it. In the former process the power of imagination has the freedom to produce intuitions that stimulate the mind to conceive of them as images with the potential to exemplify or exhibit a concept. What freedom in schematizing without concept amounts to is freedom to endow an intuition with characteristics, a specific shape or a particular figure, that make this intuition into an image that is suitable for conceptualization. In other words, the

---

[69] Cf. Kant's remark in his exchange with Eberhard (*On a Discovery*...), in which he states what he means by the term "image": "Image (which means an intuition that contains a manifold in certain relations, consequently a figure)" (AA 8, 201 f.).

activity the power of imagination carries out in the act of schematizing without concept consists in providing the means for the
transformation of an intuition into an image for which a concept
introduced by the understanding can be found.[70]

This process of schematizing without a concept can be illustrated
with an example from everyday life.[71] While sitting at my desk, even
when I am not paying particular attention to any of the things in front
of me, I have a bunch of perceptions in the sense of conscious
impressions that are independently, though disconnectedly present
to me. They form an intuitive whole without representing any specific shape. Though this whole is an intuition, it is not at this point an
image yet. Now the power of imagination brings together some of
these perceptions contained in this intuitive whole into the representation of a black, slightly elliptical, longish something.
The something thus formed is an as yet concept-less intuition that

[70] I am well aware that my reconstruction does not do justice to the intricacies of
this process, as Kant conceives it. For example, I do not mention one of Kant's
main actors in this process, namely, the power of judgment. Obviously, Kant's
emphasis that the freedom of the power of imagination consists in schematizing without concept is meant to address a situation in which the power of
judgment is involved. If we stay inside the framework in which Kant presents
his views, then to be free in the process of schematizing without a concept
would mean to be able to produce *for the sake of the power of judgment*
intuitions that can function as images, which in turn give rise to sensible
rules that are responsive to (or at least point toward) what the power of
judgment takes to be purposive for the ends of the understanding, which is
to find a concept for a hitherto concept-less intuitive item (cf., e.g., *AA* 5, 279).
It would involve attributing to the power of imagination the ability to produce
intuitions that are appraised by the power of judgment to have the potential,
either to become images of conceptualized representations, or to serve as
sensible rules for the establishment of conceptualized representations. But
because the power of judgment has to rely on the products of the power of
imagination in order to connect sensible intuitions to conceptual representations the understanding generates, the entire process of freely schematizing in
the end takes place *for the sake of the understanding*. For this reason I felt
justified in excluding the power of judgment from my reconstruction.

[71] I am focusing only on a situation in which the intuition that the power of
imagination produces can be seen as an image for which a concept is indeed
available. This differs from cases where an image is already present. In such
cases schematization already took place.

represents a certain figure. As such, it automatically qualifies for the status of an image, though not necessarily of an image for which I can find a concept. I happen to direct my attention toward this image, in order to find out to which object it refers, or maybe whether it is a representation of an object in the first place. To put this in Kantian terms, when I thus direct my attention, I am appraising [*beurteilen*] the potential of this intuitive item to be brought under a concept. This appraising is executed by my power of judgment as the capacity to decide whether this item is conceptualizable or not. If the power of judgment fails to acknowledge this potential, then the item remains a blind intuition for me, though it represents a spatiotemporal whole with a certain shape. If the power of judgment sees some potential for conceptualizing the item at hand, then it appraises the item to be purposive for the ends of the understanding. Everything depends on what the power of imagination presents to the power of judgment as an intuition. But the power of imagination, if schematizing without concept, could come up with a lot of different intuitions that the power of judgment deems purposive, even if these intuitions all incorporate the same set of sensible data. What is decisive for the process of conceptualization is whether the power of judgment can take these intuitions to be images that can be seen as exhibiting a concept. Thus the black, slightly elliptical, longish something of which I am aware, though until this moment nothing but the result of my power of imagination's play with data, could assume (perhaps just to please the power of judgment) the shape of something that can count for the power of judgment as the image of a black pen that is gently sloping down the surface of my desk, an image that might in turn "awaken" the understanding to do some work by producing or applying the concept "pen" to it. Or the power of imagination could try to please the power of judgment by using the very same sensible material, but coming up with a shape of something that reminds the power of judgment of a black worm crawling slowly along my desk, thereby stirring the understanding to set to work with the concept "worm."

Both cases show that one has to acknowledge, (1) that the power of imagination schematizes or provides a schema in the form of an image without a concept; (2) that the power of imagination can "choose" between many different alternatives as to how to schematize a given manifold of sensible data and is in this sense "free" in pursuing its concept-less schematizing activity; (3) that this schematizing in the end takes place for the sake of the power of judgment, which is in turn active on behalf of the understanding, and; (4) that the successful establishment of an intuition that counts as an image, for which a concept could be found, might be accompanied by a feeling of pleasure, thus giving rise to an aesthetic experience.

As I admitted, there are alternative ways of reconstructing what Kant means by schematizing without concept, but these are irrelevant for our purposes. Our reason for examining what Kant has to say about the power of imagination in the third *Critique* was not to exhaust his considerations concerning the conditions of an aesthetic judgment, but to find out whether the third *Critique* can give us clues into the workings of the power of imagination in the process of forming representations of objects. We will not be surprised to discover that, once this process is conceived of along the lines we pursued, this is indeed the case.

In the beginning we acknowledged that there have been serious doubts about the power of imagination as a constitutive and self-standing factor in Kant's attempt to bring together conceptual and nonconceptual elements in his conception of an object of cognition as outlined in the *CpR*. But it the end we can see that these doubts lose their ground, if one is prepared to follow the suggestions I proposed. As I take myself to have shown, the power of imagination in fact carries the main burden in the laborious process of turning amorphous and unstructured physiological sense impressions into representations of full-blown cognitive objects. In the initial sensory stages of this process, the power of imagination plays a surprisingly autonomous role and reveals an admirable and almost unrestrained range of creative activities, whose rules (if there are any) are unknown to us. It is only in the later, conceptual stages of this process that the power of imagination has to submit to foreign demands and follow the categorial rules of the understanding. All this confirms Kant's own assessment of the power of imagination, according to which it is "a blind, though indispensable function of the soul, without which we would have no cognition at all" (A 78/B 103). We now have tools for explaining why Kant was ultimately right to insist on the essential role that the power of imagination has to play, even in purely epistemological contexts. It cannot be denied that he himself became increasingly reluctant to highlight this role as clearly as he did in the first edition of the *CpR*. Yet this reluctance seems to be rooted less in doubts about the power of imagination's vital function, and more in the complexities of its activities. In any case, it does not indicate that Kant changed his general view in a fundamental way.

In my presentation of how Kant could have conceived of the contribution of the power of imagination in the process of establishing the representation of an object about which valid judgments can be made, I have dealt mainly with those aspects that are relevant to the way in which the power of imagination might be thought of as working independently of though in relation to the understanding. The picture that emerges, both in the two editions of the first *Critique* and in the aesthetic part of the third *Critique*, is complicated. The power of imagination is in charge of delivering intuitions, for which it has to perform two types of operations: (a) to discern different sense impressions or sensations in order to arrive at a manifold of conscious representations (perceptions, according to the terminology of the A-edition of the *CpR*), and (b) to bring these perceptions together (synthesize them via aesthetic comprehension, according to the third *Critique*) into an intuition, an intuitive whole. In performing both of these operations, the power of imagination is free, albeit to varying degrees (cf. p. 42), in that it is not bound by any rules of the understanding. The power of imagination performs these operations on the level of sensibility, and generates an intuition that is undetermined in regard to whether it is the representation of a specific cognitive object. At this level, the intuition is just a representation of what Kant calls an "appearance," "an undetermined object" (A 20/B 34). This is so because at this level no conceptual actions by the understanding are involved in the process of synthesizing perceptions into intuitions. But even though the power of imagination enjoys enormous freedom in its production of intuitions, not just from the understanding, but from any "outside" intervention (since it is subject only to the conditions of time and the unity of apperception), it can use this freedom to relate "voluntarily" to those conceptual activities of the understanding aiming at determining representations of objects via concepts, as Kant emphasizes and elaborates in the third *Critique*. It realizes this "voluntary" relation to the understanding when it supports the understanding in its efforts to find sensible material that fits the categorial requirements for establishing a representation of an object. And it accomplishes this by providing schemata or "schematizing without concept." One can think of the introduction of the idea of schematizing without concept in the third *Critique* as a belated acknowledgment on Kant's part that even in cognitive contexts the power of imagination must play an autochthonous and original role. The relevant passages in the third *Critique* can be read as Kant's attempt to elaborate how the power of imagination is supposed to work, not under the dominion of the understanding, but with a view to its needs.[72]

---

[72] One might wonder why I did not mention Kant's considerations concerning aesthetic ideas as presented in the third *Critique* in the reconstruction I have here attempted. This can seem like a grave omission, given the fact that Kant repeatedly emphasizes the freedom the power of imagination enjoys in its intuition-producing capacity (cf., e.g., *AA* 5. 314, 316 f.) in the course of these considerations. But a closer look shows that his views about aesthetic ideas are not meant to shed light on the function of the power of imagination in cognitive contexts. On the contrary, he explicitly states: "An *aesthetic idea* cannot become a cognition, because it is an *intuition* (of the power of imagination) for which no concept can ever be found adequate" (*AA* 5, 342). It is an "inexponible representation" (ibid., 343) of the power of imagination, a representation that resists conceptualization. As such, an aesthetic idea has the same status as a blind intuition. The difference is that, whereas a blind intuition resists conceptualization because it contains less than is necessary to capture it with a concept, an aesthetic idea resists conceptualization because it contains much more than can ever be captured with a concept [*auf einen Begriff bringen*] (cf. ibid., 314, 343). Though Kant's conception of an aesthetic idea is undoubtedly of interest as a part of his aesthetic theory, it has no genuine connection to the task pursued here, namely to work out in detail Kant's conception of the way in which the power of imagination is supposed to contribute to cognition.

This Element is dedicated to Paul and Béatrice

Cambridge Elements ≡

# The Philosophy of Immanuel Kant

## Desmond Hogan
*Princeton University*
Desmond Hogan joined the philosophy department at Princeton in 2004. His interests include Kant, Leibniz and German rationalism, early modern philosophy, and questions about causation and freedom. Recent work includes Kant on Foreknowledge of Contingent Truths, *Res Philosophica* 91 (1) (2014); 'Kant's Theory of Divine and Secondary Causation,' in Brandon Look (ed.) *Leibniz and Kant*, Oxford University Press (forthcoming); 'Kant and the Character of Mathematical Inference,' in *Kant's Philosophy of Mathematics Vol. I*, Carl Posy and Ofra Rechter (eds.), Cambridge University Press (forthcoming).


## Howard Williams
*University of Cardiff*
Howard Williams was appointed Honorary Distinguished Professor at the Department of Politics and International Relations, University of Cardiff in 2014. He is also Emeritus Professor in Political Theory at the Department of International Politics, Aberystwyth University, a member of the Coleg Cymraeg Cenedlaethol (Welsh language national college) and a Fellow of the Learned Society of Wales. He is the author of *Marx* (1980); *Kant's Political Philosophy* (1983); *Concepts of Ideology* (1988); *International Relations in Political Theory* (1992); *Hegel, Heraclitus and Marx's Dialectic; International Relations and the Limits of Political Theory* (1996); *Kant's Critique of Hobbes: Sovereignty and Cosmopolitanism* (2003), *Kant and the end of War* (2012) and is currently editor of the journal *Kantian Review*. He is writing a book on the Kantian Legacy in Political Philosophy for a new series edited by Paul Guyer.


## Allen Wood
*Indiana University*
Allen Wood is Ward W. and Pricilla B. Woods Professor at Stanford University. He was a John S. Guggenheim Fellow at the Free University in Berlin, a national Endowment for the Humanities Fellow at the University of Bonn and Isaiah Berlin Visiting Professor at the University of Oxford. He is on the editorial board of eight philosophy journals, five book series and the Stanford Encyclopedia of Philosophy. Along with Paul Guyer, Professor Wood is co-editor of the Cambridge Edition of the Works of Immanuel Kant and translator of the Critique of Pure Reason. He is the author or editor of a number of other works, mainly on Kant, Hegel and Karl Marx. His most recently published book, *Fichte's Ethical Thought*, was published by Oxford University Press in 2016. Wood is a member of the American Academy of Arts and Sciences.

## About the series
This Elements series on *The Philosophy of Immanuel Kant* provides an extensive overview of Kant's philosophy and its impact upon philosophy and philosophers. Distinguished Kant specialists provide an up to date summary of the results of current research in their fields and give their own take on what they believe are the most significant debates influencing research, drawing original conclusions.

Printed in the United States
By Bookmasters